WAKEFIELD'S MILITARY HERITAGE

Paul L. Dawson

AMBERLEY

First published 2025

Amberley Publishing
The Hill, Stroud
Gloucestershire, GL5 4EP

www.amberley-books.com

Logo source material courtesy of Gerry van Tonder

ISBN 978 1 3981 2127 0 (print)
ISBN 978 1 3981 2128 7 (ebook)

British Library Cataloguing in Publication Data.
A catalogue record for this book is available from the British Library.

Origination by Amberley Publishing.
Printed in Great Britain.

Appointed GPSR EU Representative: Easy Access System Europe Oü, 16879218
Address: Mustamäe tee 50, 10621, Tallinn, Estonia
Contact Details: gpsr.requests@easproject.com, +358 40 500 3575

Contents

Introduction and Acknowledgements

This book is a family effort. The first two chapters are from the research and notes made by my mother, Jane Dawson, née Cresswell (1953–2008), who was studying for a Master of Arts degree – 'Richard Duke of York (1411–1460) and the Politics which Led to the Battle of Wakefield'. My own research, as part of the Newlands Project by Wakefield Historical Society, forms the core of chapter 3. My twin, Anthony Leslie Dawson, has graciously allowed his research and reassessment of the siege of Sandal Castle to be abridged into the chapter, and our joint research into volunteer and auxiliary forces of Wakefield, commenced over twenty-five years ago, forms chapter 5. Our last chapter relies heavily on my own family's experience of war, as well as the research of Dr P. Judkins, a lifelong friend and mentor.

Readers may well be critical of what I have included, and even omitted, from this book, but I hope it brings to the fore the importance of Wakefield's military heritage, and how the events of 1460 transformed the history of the nation as much as Wakefield lass Barbara Dixon did.

This book does not seek to give a chapter and verse history of Wakefield; the author's other books, notably *Wakefield: A Potted History*, do that. Instead, this book seeks to give an outline of key persons and events from or associated with Wakefield that have contributed to the military heritage of our city. It does not rely on nostalgia but, rather, aims to tell the story of how Wakefield has been shaped by, and contributed to, military feats of arms.

Paul L. Dawson

1. Of Castles and Kings

The skyline south of Wakefield is dominated by the ruined castle at Sandal. It is the oldest military installation in the city and was built by some of the greatest soldiers of the Middle Ages, the Warenne family.

The town of Varenne, near Dieppe in north-east Normandy, was the home town of the earl. The first known member of the family is Ralph de Warenne in the 1030s, but the family's advancement and enrichment was through his son William's active support of William, Duke of Normandy, in the mid-1050s. His reward for loyalty included the gift of a place upstream on Varenne called Bennecombre, where he built a massive motte-and-bailey castle. This remained the headquarters of the family in Normandy until 1204, and of the Norman branch until 1261. After 1066, William de Warenne became one of the many European elites whose fortunes were transformed by the conquest of England; William fought at Hastings and was one of William the Conqueror's inner political circle. Indeed, he was one of the four magnates who ruled in William I's absence in 1067.

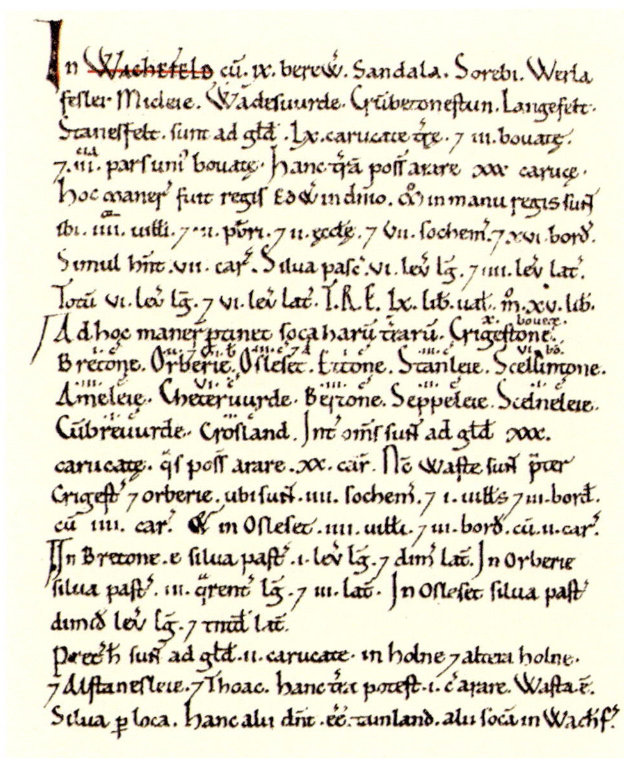

Wakefield's entry in the Domesday Book, the first written record of the city.

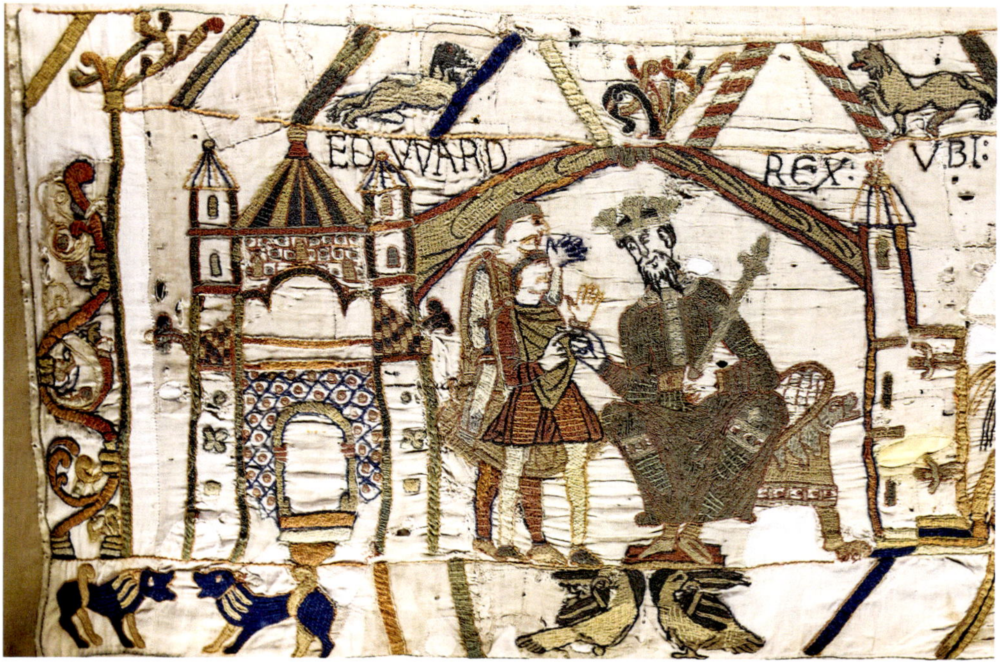

The first scene of the Bayeaux Tapestry, showing King Edward the Confessor.

By May 1070, William de Warenne had been given the 'rape of Lewes', a large swathe of southern England vulnerable to attack from the troublesome dukes of Flanders and Boulogne. This was a task given only to William I's most trusted allies. Warenne gained land in Norfolk through marriage to Gundrada (of Norse origin), sister and heir of Frederick, who had received estates that included what is now Castle Acre by 1071. He enlarged his landholdings in 1075 as a reward for supressing a revolt in East Anglia.

After William I's death in 1087, Warenne supported William Rufus (r. 1087–1100) against William I's rebellious half-brother, Bishop Odo of Bayeux, and Robert of Mortain. He was rewarded with more land in Sussex and Surrey, being created Earl of Surrey. Warenne was described by a near contemporary as 'warlike, fierce in spirit, strong in body and distinguished in fame'. He met his end, however, during the siege of Pevensy Castle in 1088, held by Robert of Mortain, when he was struck in the eye by an arrow. Warenne's body was carried to Lewes where he died shortly afterwards; he was buried in Lewes Priory.

He was succeeded by William, 2nd Earl of Surrey (the first to style himself as Earl Warenne), who had a career as a soldier and politician on par with his father. When Wiliam Rufus was killed by accident or murdered – it is hard to say – his younger and ruthless brother Henry took the throne. Civil war ensued and Warenne took the side of Robert Curthose when he landed in England in 1101 to oust his brother. The invasion failed and Warenne forfeited his lands. Seeking to win royal favour and regain his lands, Warenne changed sides and fought by Henry I's side at Tinchebray in 1106. This was not the end of the vicious civil war that engulfed England and Normandy. Robert Curthoses's son, William Clito, almost succeeded in establishing himself as Count of Flanders in 1127. It was his death a year later that ended the war. Now an intimate of the royal circle, Warenne was frequently in the king's company and was celebrated for his loyalty. He was rewarded with lands in Yorkshire, which included the manor of Wakefield, Conisbrough and Tickhill, as well as more estates in Normandy. Warenne married Isabel de Vermandois in 1118, who had been recently widowed. According to one chronicle, by the time of their marriage she had already been living with Warenne for some years, 'stolen by intrigue and treachery'.

It was on William de Warenne, 2nd Earl of Surrey's initiative that work began to construct a motte-and-bailey castle near Wakefield at Sandal. It was also the 2nd Earl who granted Robert de Flemming the power to found a Cistercian nunnery at Kirklees. William founded no other monastic institution in the manor; instead, he invested heavily at his priories at Lewes and Castle Acre, where great stone castles arose. This perhaps reflects Warenne's ambivalent attitude to the small, impoverished village of Wakefield. At Castle Acre, Warenne built both a Cluniac monastery, laid out a new town and invested in the stone castle. At Sandal, a simple timber hall and tower was deemed sufficient. Perhaps fifty men or fewer were garrisoned in the castle.

Presumably the castle at Sandal was completed by Warenne's death in 1138. He was succeeded by his son, another William, the 3rd Earl, who died on crusade in 1148.

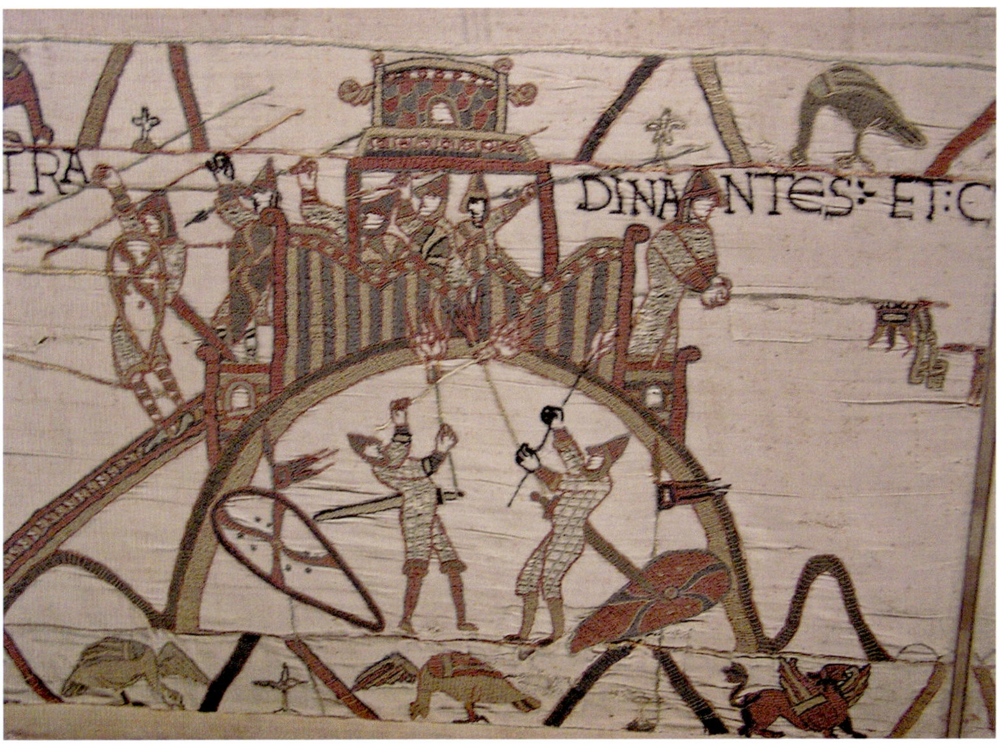

On coming to Wakefield, we assume the Normans built the motte-and-bailey castle in Thornes Park. It would have looked something like this example at Dinantes from the Bayeaux Tapestry. The castle at Thornes remained in use until 1322, by which time a new and large location had been found at Sandal.

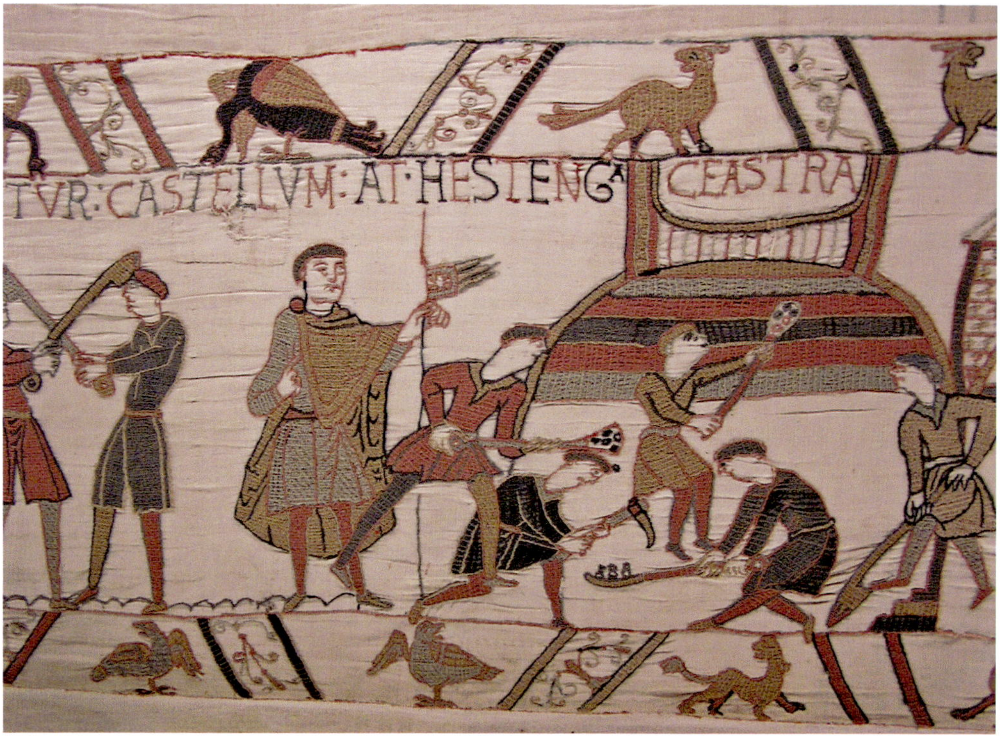

This scene from the Bayeaux Tapestry shows workmen busily building a great earthen mound to form a motte, on which a watchtower was erected.

He deserted King Stephen (r. 1135–54) when the latter endeavoured to invade Normandy. Like his father, he changed sides after seeing which way the wind was blowing, and aided Stephen during the civil war with Empress Matilda, who had been named heir by her father, Henry I. Upon the 3rd Earl's death near Laodicea in modern Turkey, at the side of King Louis VII of France and surrounded by the Knights Templar, his estates passed to his daughter Isabel, and thus, with the earldoms of Surrey and Warenne, to her husband, William of Blois, King Stephen's youngest son. It was probably the 3rd Earl who gave land in Alverthorpe to the Knights Templar, where they established a preceptory and farm, which boasted a water mill and over 200 acres of land.

During these turbulent times the motte-and-bailey castle in Thornes Park may have been erected. It could have been built by William II before his death or by Isabel. The war between Stephen and Matilda, known as the Anarchy, left Yorkshire almost unscathed. Therefore, the need for a castle is rather odd, as the closest the fighting came was far to the south in Lincoln. In 1153 Stephen and Matilda came to an agreement that Henry of Anjou, Matilda's eldest son, would be his successor. William of Blois, 4th Earl of Surrey and Count of Boulogne, was excluded from the line of succession.

When William of Blois died in 1159, Henry II (r. 1154–89) decreed that William's sister, Mary, would inherit the Boulogne title and other estates, and then gave her in marriage to Matthew of Alsace, younger brother to Philip, Count of Flanders. The marriage was problematic as Mary was abbess of Romsey Priory. Isabel married Hamelin Plantagenet in 1164, half-brother of Henry II, making him 5th Earl of Surrey. Hamelin was a loyal supporter of Henry II in the struggles with his kith and kin.

In 1167 both Philip, Count of Flanders, and his brother Matthew supported King Louis of France against Henry II and their kinsman, Hamelin. They threatened to invade Kent, but were handsomely paid off by Henry II. The two brothers joined Henry II's eldest son, Henry 'the Young King', who had been crowned King of England but was never allowed to rule. The Young King paid them £1,000 a year and they were given lands in Kent and the castles of Dover and Rochester in reward for their invasion of Normandy. The Young King was supported by his brothers Geoffrey, Duke of Brittany, and Richard 'the Lionheart' as well as by their mother Eleanor of Aquitaine. Matthew was killed in fighting at Drincourt in July 1173 and Philip, Count of Flanders, invaded England. He assembled a fleet at Wissant and Gravelines, then captured Norwich on 18 June 1174. The revolt was joined by the King of Scotland and other allies in what became known as the Great Revolt. Peace was brokered in 1175, but the Young King again rose in revolt in 1183, during which he died. Geoffrey was accidentally 'killed' – murdered seems more likely – in 1186, which brought Henry II some peace. This was shattered by Richard and John rising in rebellion in 1189. Henry II died on campaign fighting his sons and Richard (r. 1189–99) became king. With Hamelin heavily invested in fighting he found little time or finances to spend at Sandal, but he did invest at Conisbrough, building the great keep in imitation of that at Gisors, Vexin, France, then over forty years old.

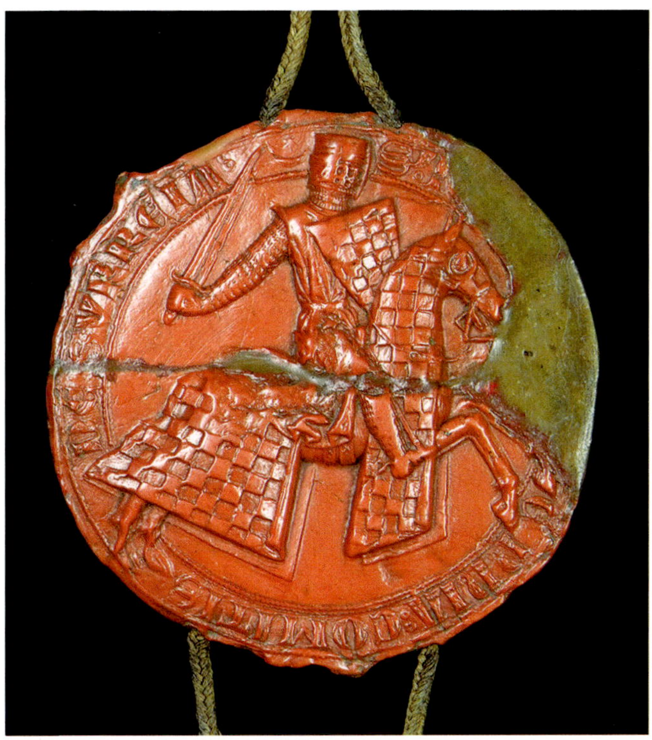

Great seal of John de Warenne, 6th Earl of Surrey.

Hamelin's son, William Plantagenet, 5th Earl of Surrey, inherited his father's estates in 1202 during the troubled reign of King John (r. 1199–1216). The earl probably never travelled to Sandal; he was pre-occupied by his duties in the south. His first tenure of office, as Lord Warden of the Cinque Ports, began in 1204 and lasted until 1206. He was appointed as warden again in 1214. He was also a warden of the Welsh Marches between 1208 and 1213. Between the years 1200 and 1208, and between 1217 and 1226, he was to serve as the high sheriff of Surrey. During King John's difficulties with the barons, William is listed as one of those who advised John to accede to Magna Carta. John promptly had it annulled by the pope. William's allegiance only faltered when the king's cause looked hopeless. The barons invited the French king to invade and captured, among other places, both Rochester and Windsor castles, and laid siege to Dover and Lincoln. Had it not been for William Marshal acting to defend the English crown at the Battle of Lincoln, Prince Louis of France may well have been King of England. In March 1217 Warenne switched sides and supported the young King Henry III (r. 1216–72). William married Maud Marshal, daughter of William Marshall and widow of Hugh Bigod, 3rd Earl of Norfolk, on 13 October 1225. They had one son, John, and a daughter, Isabel. John (1231–1304) succeeded his father as earl, while Isabel (*c.* 1228–82) married Hugh d'Aubigny, 5th Earl of Arundel. William may also have had an earlier childless marriage to another Maud, daughter of William d'Aubigny, 2nd Earl of Arundel. William disliked the royal favourites who came into power after 1227 and changed sides again, and by 1238 he was regarded as a leader of the baronial opposition. He died in May 1240. It may have been this William who began building the stone castle at Sandal, commencing with the keep, which was very reminiscent of those in France constructed over 100 years earlier. An inquisition of 1240 on the earl's death is the first document that mentions the castle and town of Sandal – presumably this was a formally laid out new town.

It was during the life of John, 6th Earl of Surrey and Warenne, that the stone castle was completed. John was a boy when his father died and, with Peter of Savoy appointed guardian of his holdings, he was raised at the royal court. In 1247, he married the king's half-sister, Alicia de Lusignan, further reinforcing the family's longstanding royal connections. A significant soldier and statesmen, in 1254 Warenne accompanied the king's son Edward (the future Edward I) on his journey to Spain to marry Eleanor of Castile. During the conflicts between Henry III and his barons, Warenne started as a strong supporter of the king, switched to support for Simon de Montfort, and then returned to the royalist party. He opposed the initial baronial reform plan of May 1258, but along with other opponents capitulated and took the oath of the Provisions of Oxford. By 1260, Warenne had joined the party of Simon de Montfort, but switched back to the king's side in 1263. In April 1264, he and Roger de Leybourne were besieged by de Montfort at Rochester Castle. In May of the same year Warenne was present for the Battle of Lewes (fought near his ancestral home, Lewes Castle). After the capture of the king and Prince Edward he fled to the Continent, where he remained for about a year. His estates were confiscated but were subsequently restored. He returned to fight in the campaign which culminated in the Battle of Evesham, the Battle of Chesterfield and the siege of Kenilworth Castle.

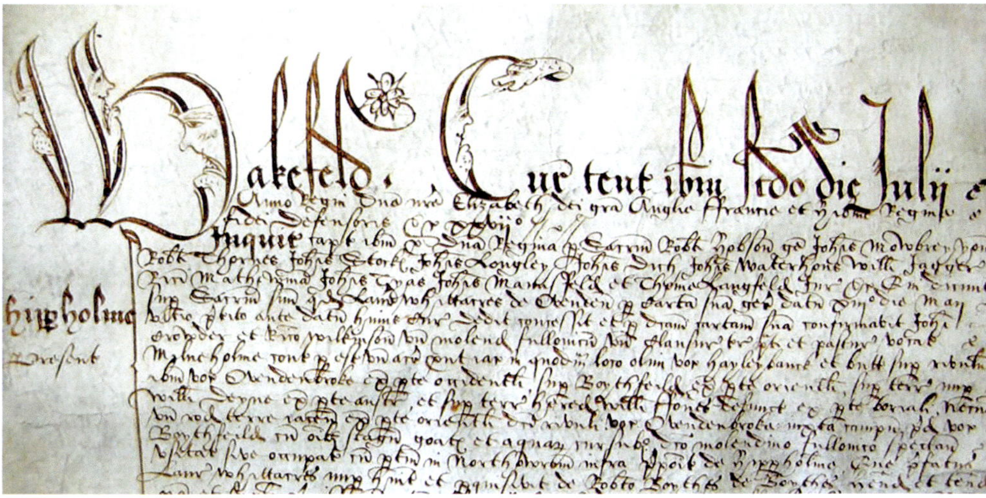

Extract from the manor of Wakefield court roll, a unique collection of international importance that is, alas, almost totally unknown and recognised in Wakefield. These records are some of the most important documents concerning the Middle Ages anywhere in the world.

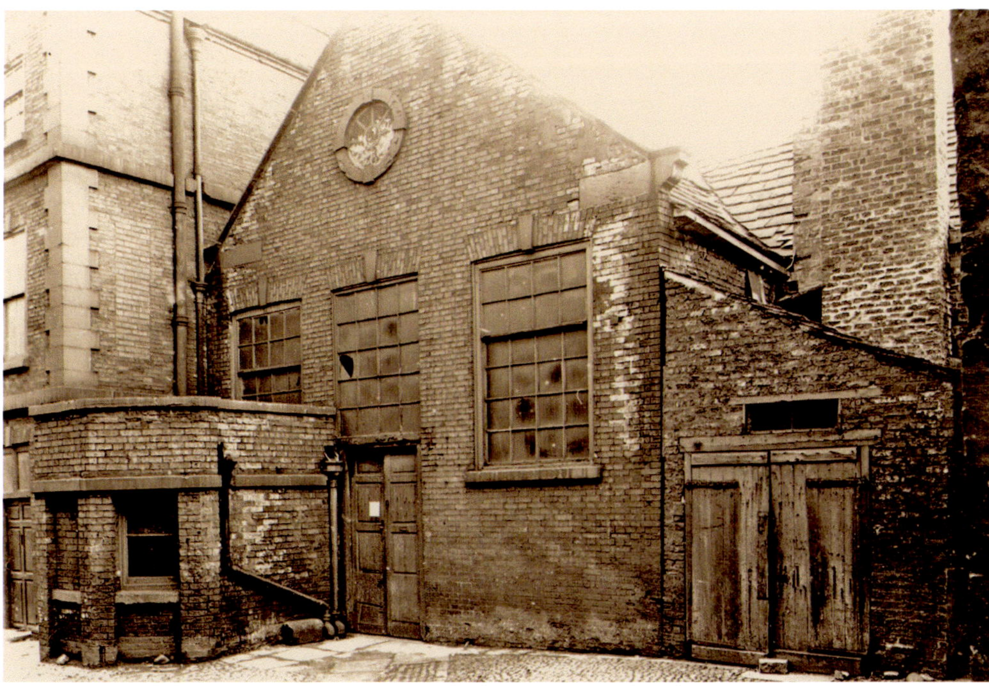

The Moot Hall once stood in Kirkgate. It was here from 1539 that the manor court rolls were lodged, and the manor court held after it had been transferred from Sandal Castle. The Moot Hall was built on the site of the great hall of Wakefield Manor House. A vast timber barn-like structure, surrounded by lodging chambers, a kitchen, blacksmith and other buildings, once dominated upper Kirkgate where Boots now stands. The Moot Hall and any traces of the medieval manor were swept away in the 1960s, with no records made of the hall or archaeology.

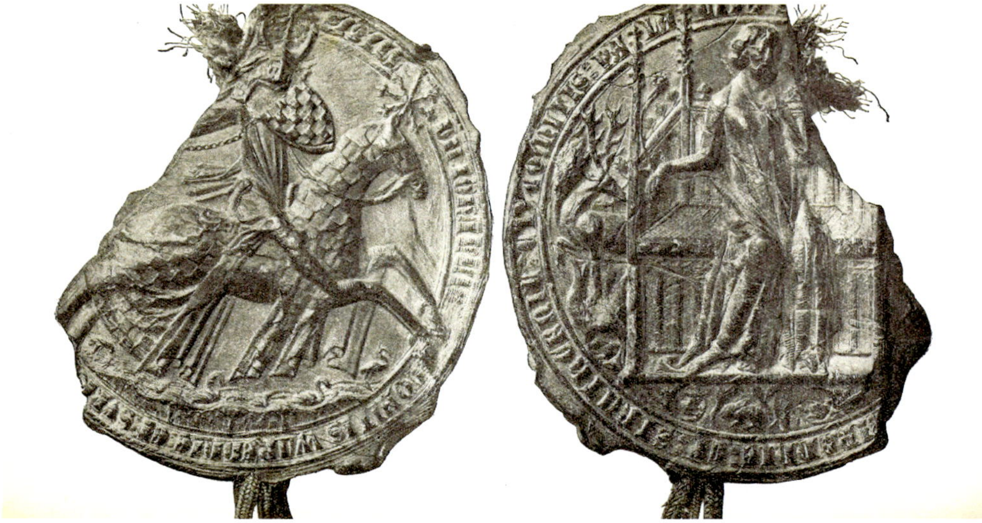

The great seal of John de Warenne, 7th Earl of Surrey.

Warenne served in the Welsh campaigns of Edward I (r. 1272–1307) in 1277, 1282, and 1283. In 1282, King Edward awarded him the lordship of Bromfield and Yale in Wales, which was taken from Prince Gruffudd Fychan I and his son Madog Crypl. He was one of the negotiators for the 1289 treaty of Salisbury and for the 1290 treaty of Birgham, and accompanied the king on Edward's 1296 invasion of Scotland where he commanded the only major field action of that year in the Battle of Dunbar, following which he was named warden of Scotland in August 1296. The following spring saw the rebellion of William Wallace. Warenne was ordered to lead his army north by the king after initially refusing to return to Scotland. He was defeated by Wallace at the Battle of Stirling Bridge and fled to York.

Nevertheless, the king appointed Warenne captain of the next campaign against the Scots in early 1298. He raised the siege of Roxburgh and retook the town of Berwick. The king himself took the field later that year and Warenne was one of the commanders during the decisive English victory at the Battle of Falkirk. During the campaign of 1300, Warenne was again in the field. On 8 August, near the estuary of the Cree, Edward ordered his men and Warenne's to charge at a Scottish force, causing the Scots to flee. He died in 1304 aged seventy-three. How much time he spent at Sandal is unclear. Warenne spent 1285–97 at Castle Acre where he welcomed Edward I five times. Certainly, it was he who commended the building of the barbican tower in 1270–71.

John's heir, his grandson and namesake, 7th Earl of Surrey and the last Earl of Warenne was an altogether different man. John's father, William, had died in 1283 whilst participating in a tournament in Croyden. A minor when his grandfather died, his lands were taken into the custody of the Crown and he was made a ward of Edward I. He was knighted on 22 May 1306 at Westminster Abbey along with 266 others, among which included the Prince of Wales, the future Edward II, and had his titles restored to him. John was one of the great nobles offended by the rise of Edward II's favourite Piers Gaveston, and he helped secure Gaveston's 1308 banishment. The two were somewhat reconciled

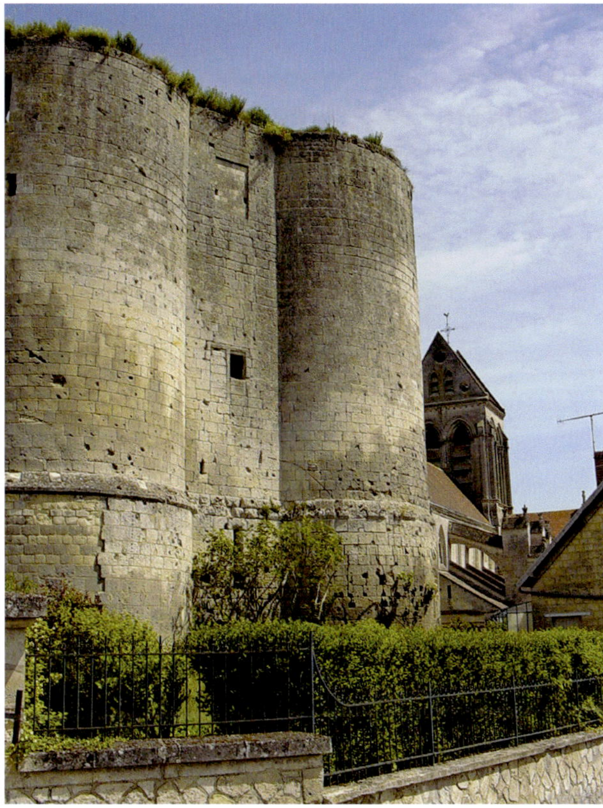

Right and below: Sandal Castle was built in earth and timber sometime before 1138. During the 1250s the earls Warenne rebuilt the castle in stone. As a Norman family, their inspiration lay in French military architecture. The great keep at Sandal was based on military architecture that was over 100 years old and inspired this great keep at Ambleny in the Aisne.

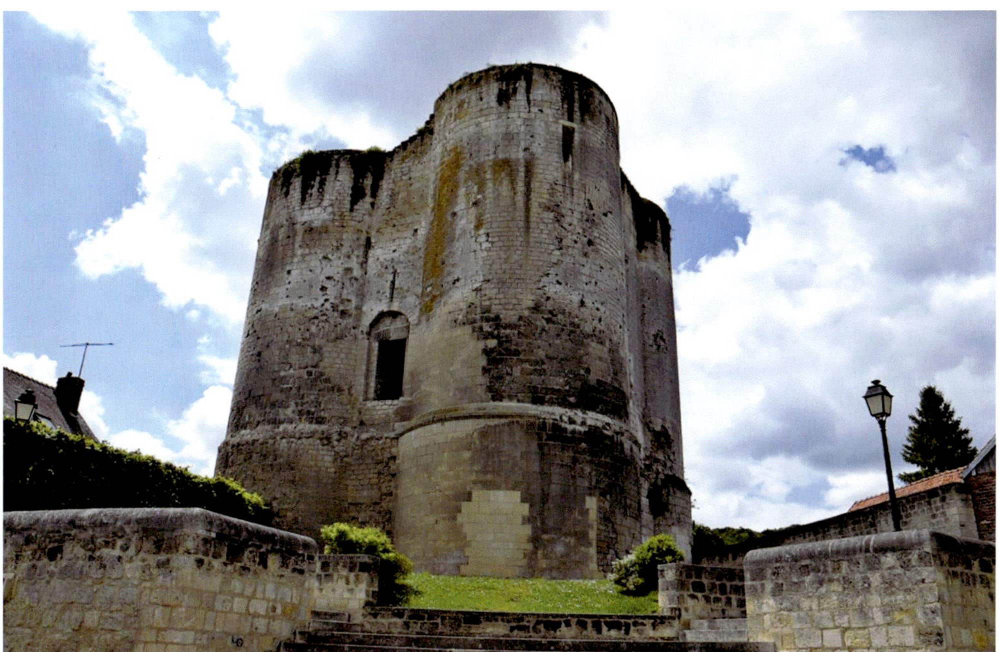

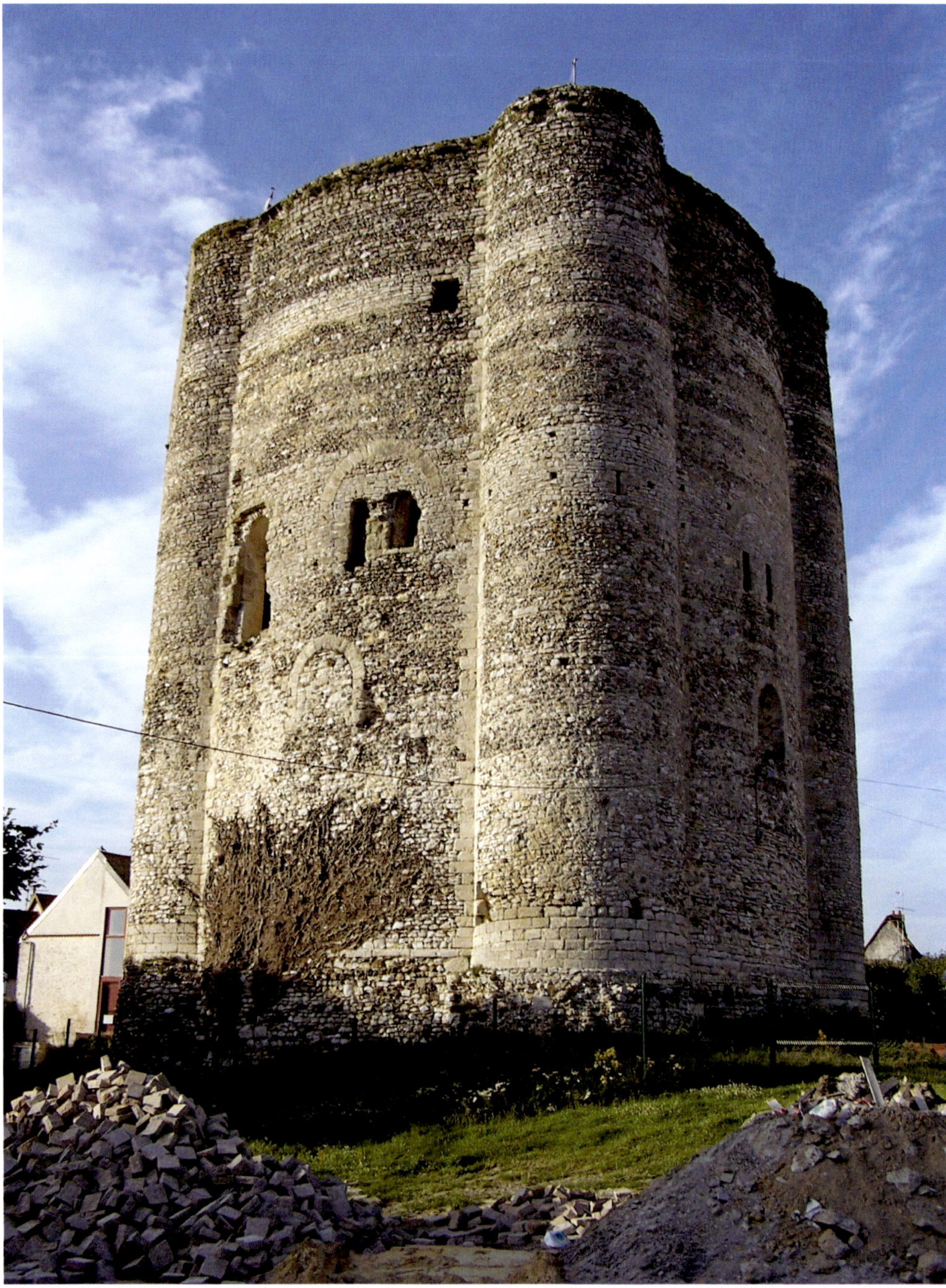

Above and opposite page: The closest parallel to the great keep at Sandal is the keep at Houdan, standing to almost full height and completed by 1140. The rebuilding at Sandal was contemporary with the new castle being built at York, Clifford's Tower, which again shares a lobed design that was based on French ideas. Houdan, in the region of Paris, has recently been conserved and opened to visitors. For those wishing to experience what the great keep at Sandal was like, this is *the* place to visit.

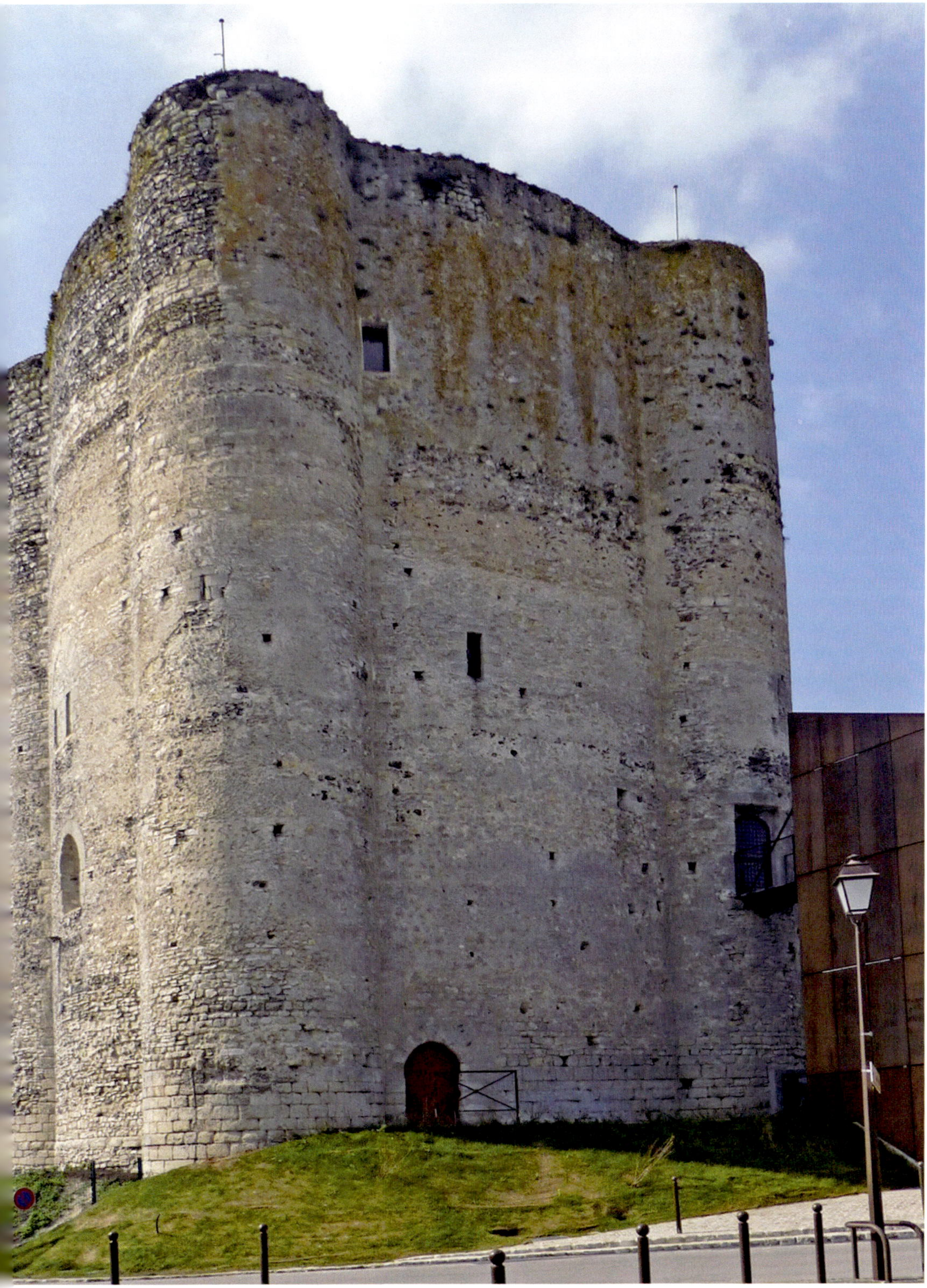

after Gaveston's return the next year, but in 1312 Warenne was one of the nobles who captured Gaveston. He was, however, unhappy about Gaveston's execution at the behest of the Earl of Warwick, which pushed him back into the king's camp. He played a risky game, constantly switching sides and alienating Thomas of Lancaster, the king's cousin, in what became a bloody feud. Sandal seems to have been attacked – perhaps besieged – in 1317, but we cannot say if the castle was seriously damaged or not. In 1319, the king granted the Earl of Lancaster the towns of Conisbrough and Sandal, along with the manors of Wakefield, Thorne, Hatfield, Sowerby, Braithwell, Fishlake, Dewsbury and Halifax. They were restored in 1326, four years after Lancaster's execution for rebellion against Edward II, following defeat at the Battle of Boroughbridge. The document also mentions 'Wakefield Castle', presumably Lowe Hill, showing the site was in use from *c.* 1130 for 200 years.

Warenne and his brother-in-law Edmund Fitzalan, 9th Earl of Arundel, were the last two earls to remain loyal to Edward II (r. 1307–27) after the rise to power of Queen Isabella and Roger Mortimer. After Arundel's execution he went over to the queen's side, urging Edward II's abdication in 1327. His personal affairs were dominated by his attempts to divorce his childless wife, the king's niece, and to provide for the children of his mistress, Matilda de Narford.

Warenne died in 1347 at Conisbrough Castle. His burial took place at the Priory Church of St Pancras, Lewes. His two sons served in the Holy Land as Knights Hospitallers, giving up their titles and lands. Sandal and the manor of Wakefield passed to the Crown. It marked the end of castle development at Sandal for over 100 years.

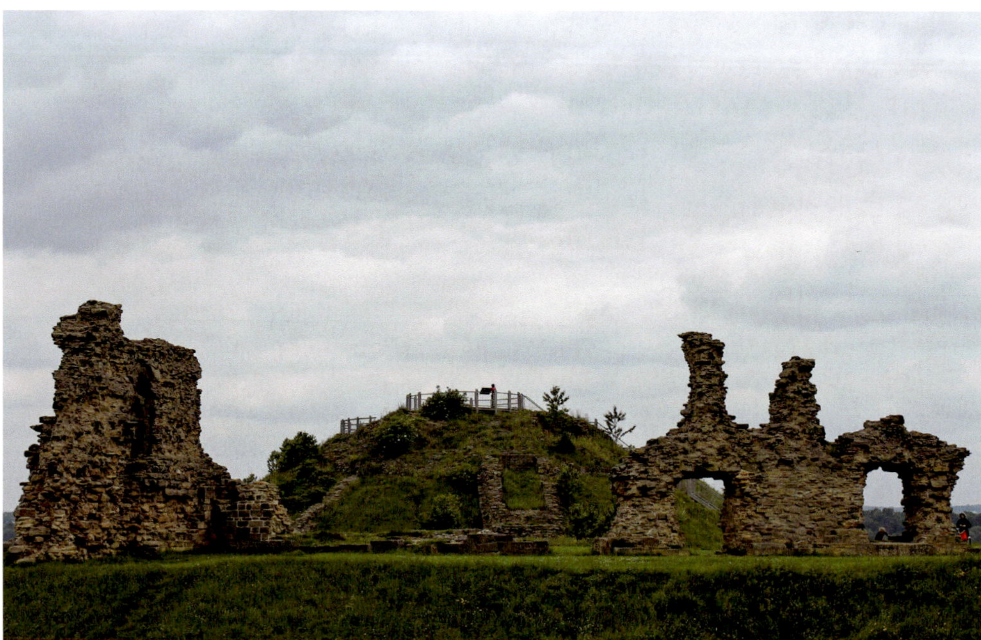

Sandal Castle as it is today, a pale reflection of its lost magnificence.

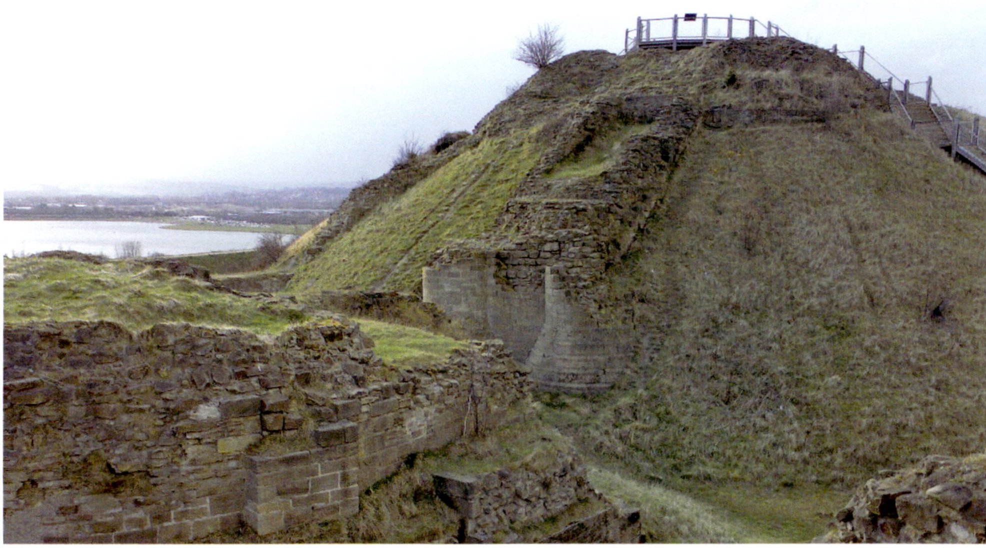

The great earthen mound on which the great keep at Sandal stood. Before the archaeological excavation of the 1960s and early 1970s, the barbican and keep gatehouse were totally buried by meters of soil and detritus.

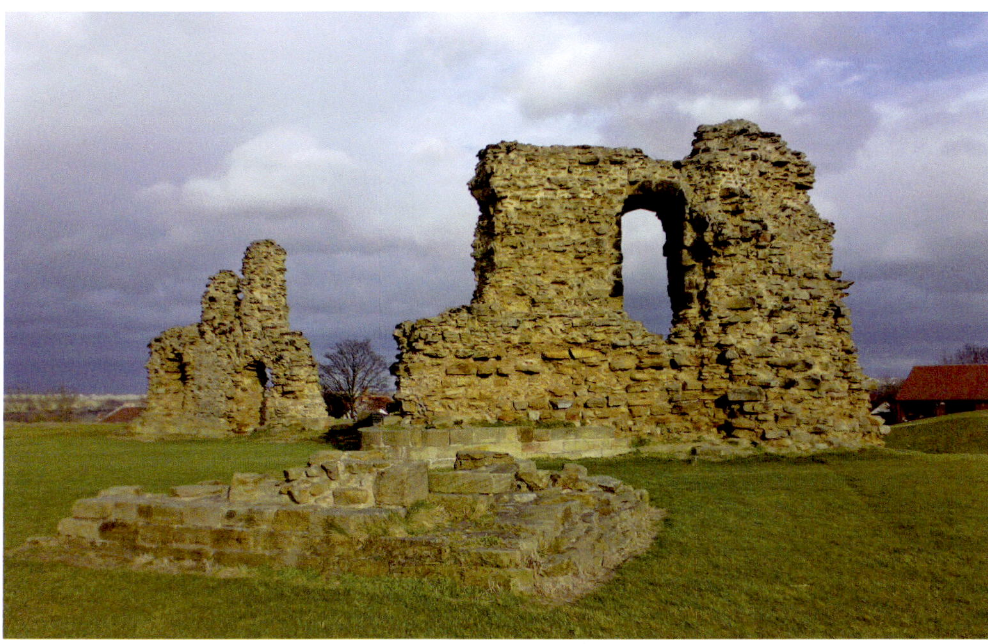

These ruined walls are all that remains of the earls Warenne's once magnificent great hall and private lodgings. Sandal was never more than a 'toy castle', however. Outdated architecturally, it sat at the centre of a vast hunting park, and by 1322 had a pleasure garden attached. The castle was a very elaborate and high-status hunting lodge for the earls Warenne, and later the Duke of York.

2. Richard, Duke of York, and the Battle of Wakefield

If Wakefield is known for any military event, it is for Richard, 3rd Duke of York's death, supposedly on 30 December 1460. The prelude to the events was the removal of Richard II (r. 1377–99) from the throne and his replacement by Henry Bolingbroke as Henry IV (r. 1399–1413). Civil war ensued, resulting in the Battle of Shrewsbury (21 July 1403), which secured his position as king. Henry IV was succeeded by his son, Henry V (r. 1413–22), who used the opportunity of war with France to unite the elite behind him – he narrowly escaped a coup lead by the earls of Masham, Northumberland, Cambridge and others in 1415, in what is known as the Southampton Plot. Interestingly, at the time of the plot the Earl of Masham was resident at Sandal Castle, and had been since 1411. He had married the widow of Edmund Langley, Duke of York. Henry V won a victory at Agincourt, which secured Lancastrian power, but his early death in 1422 and succession by his son Henry VI (r. 1422–61 and 1470–71) sparked a very real constitutional crisis, which is now known as the Wars of the Roses.

Henry VI was afflicted by acute mental health issues and proved almost incapable of rule. By 1450, the defeats and failures of the English royal government in France had boiled over into serious political unrest, known as Jack Cade's Rebellion. York made a bid for power, but not to become king himself. Protesting his loyalty, he aimed to be recognised as Henry VI's heir to the throne (at this point Henry was childless after seven years of marriage). York's grandfather was Edward III, so he had the same claim to the throne as Henry Bolingbroke, Henry IV.

At the Battle of St Albans on 22 May 1455, York killed many of the key leaders of the opposing house of Lancaster, leaving Lord Clifford, Henry Beaufort, the Earl of Somerset and others seeking revenge for their father's murder. Following the battle, Henry VI was placed into the York's custody, along with his two-year-old son. York was made constable of England. The period 1456–59 was marked by political turmoil that verged on civil war. In June 1459 a Great Council was summoned to meet at Coventry. York, the Nevilles and some other lords refused to appear, fearing that the armed forces that had been commanded to assemble the previous month had been summoned to arrest them. York was right to be concerned, for in December 1459 York and the earls of Warwick and Salisbury suffered attainder. Their lives were forfeit and their lands reverted to the king; their heirs would not inherit. This was the most extreme punishment a member of the nobility could suffer, and York was now in the same situation that Henry of Bolingbroke had been in 1398. York, now in Ireland with an army, understood that only a successful invasion of England would restore his fortune. Assuming the invasion was successful, York had three options: become protector again, disinherit the king's son so that York would succeed, or claim the throne for himself.

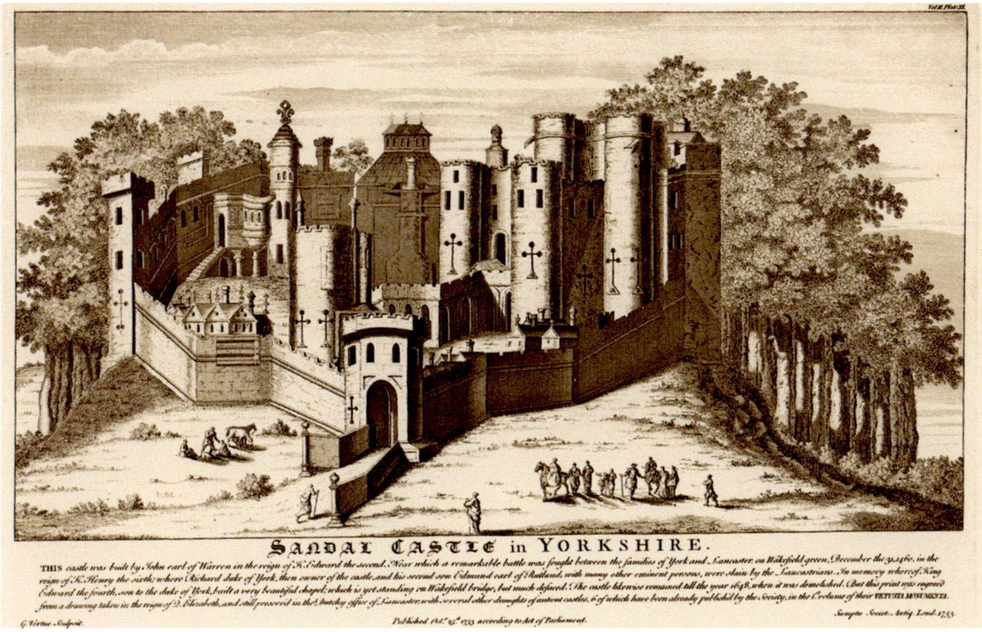

This eighteenth-century engraving is based on an image of Sandal from 1564, but bares no real resemblance to reality. The motte on which the keep stands is omitted; the barbican is reduced in scale; and the stairs from the keep gatehouse up the slope of the keep are impossible to reconcile with the castle's actual ground plan revealed through archaeology. Moreover, the castle was not surrounded by woodland, nor does it sit on a large hillock as shown. The woods shown in the image are entirely artistic licence and have led to a centuries-long myth about the Battle of Wakefield. The original ink, chalk and watercolour image housed in the National Archives, Kew, is a workshop piece. It was not drawn from life, but from sketches and notes taken in the field and then reworked. Neither image, alas, is an accurate or reliable image of Sandal.

In early summer 1460, the Earl of Warwick, backed by the Earl of Salisbury, launched one of the last successful invasions of the country – the last was arguably in 1688. It was at the head of a French army that Henry VII won the throne in 1485. Warwick's forces were bolstered by the Calais garrison – perhaps the only professional force of soldiers in the country. Warwick and Salisbury's victory at the Battle of Northampton gave them control of the hapless king. York landed from Ireland in September and proclaimed himself king. Henry VI had proven to be incapable of governance and the Lancastrian faction had become powerful and wealthy through the lack of a strong king. York blamed the loss of French possessions and the economic crisis that gripped the country on Henry VI. He hoped that by claiming the throne he could save the nation from inevitable invasion from France and Scotland. France had collapsed as a military power due to a weak king, which had allowed Henry V's conquest; the same fate for England looked imminent.

A strong king was needed to lead the nation and Henry VI was not up to the task. Parliament and the House of Lords agreed. The Act of Accord, made in the October Parliament, named Richard, 3rd Duke of York, as heir to the throne. The Act of Accord specified that any act of aggression or malice against York – or the king – would be considered treason. Queen Margaret, believing she had lost the war before it began, pleaded with her uncle, Charles VII of France, for asylum. Yet it was not to France she fled but to Scotland, accompanied by the bishops of Lichfield and Carlisle, the Earl of Exeter, the Duke of Devon and other nobles.

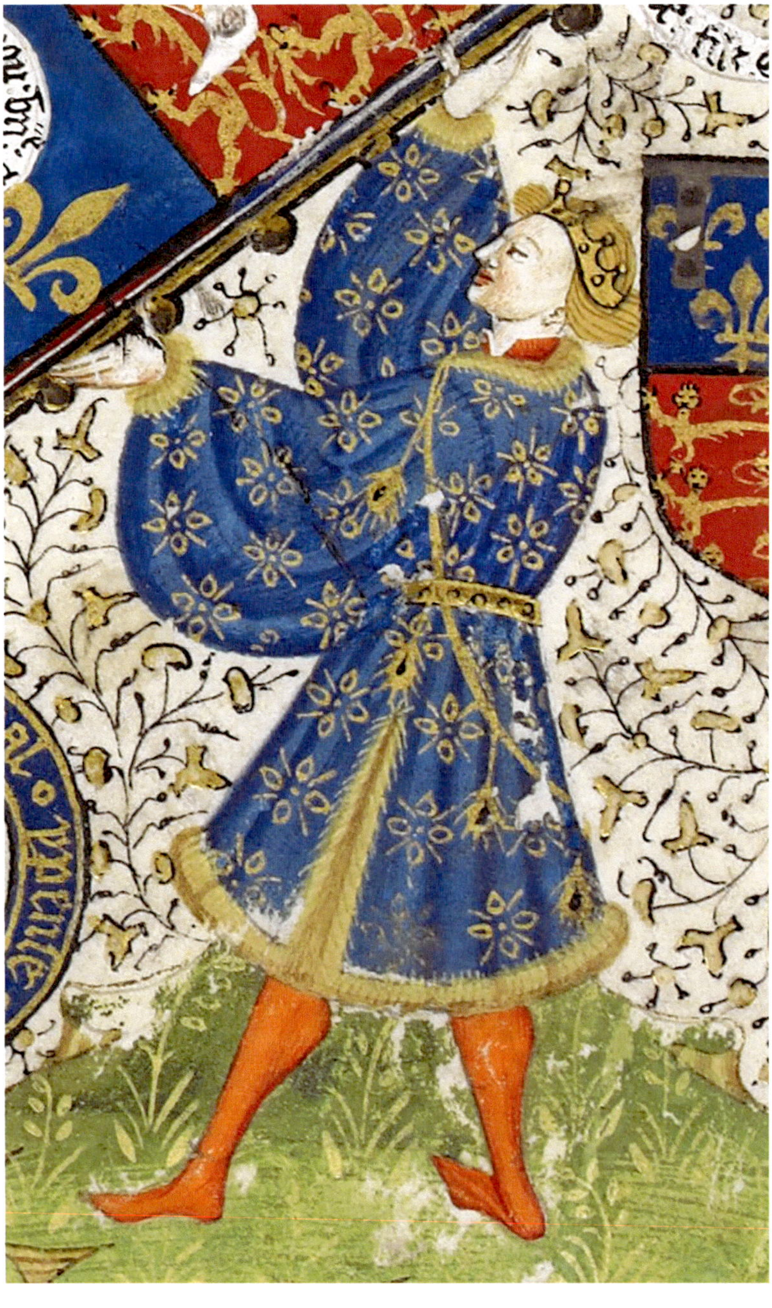

Richard, Duke of York (1411–60) was heir to the throne. His personal ambition as well as the failure of his rival, the Earl of Somerset, to retain territory won by Henry V in France and the Europe-wide economic recession led to the Wars of the Roses. His sons, Edward and Richard, became kings of England and his granddaughter became the queen of Henry VII.

In Yorkshire, the Earl of Northumberland, York's sworn enemy, had refused to accept York as heir. He began killing leading Yorkists and destroying their lands and property. Based at Pontefract Castle, the earl burned Sandal Castle to the ground, denying York a power base in the north. York was commissioned by Parliament to end Northumberland's reign of terror and destroying Sandal and ravaging the vast manor of Wakefield was an act of terror and resource denial. Both the court rolls of the manor of Wakefield and the archaeological excavation of the castle show the buildings in the bailey were destroyed by fire. The castle remained uninhabited until 1843.

To face Northumberland, who had also taken over Wressle Castle and nearby Spofforth, the Duke of York and his ally Richard Neville, Earl of Salisbury, left London in early December, a few days after Parliament had been prorogued, taking with them just a small force. York had with him his household and entourage filled with lawyers. His goal, as in 1454, was to enter York and hold petty sessions to bring the violence to an end. Protected by the law of treason, York felt himself invincible. York arrived in Wakefield on Christmas Day 1460 to find Sandal a smoking ruin – we think he arrived from Conisbrough. He ejected the small garrison left by the Earl of Northumberland and appointed his own officers to run the manor. Lodging in the precursor to the Moot Hall, the Earls Hall or medieval manor house of the then town, records of the manor of Wakefield (inscribed on the UNESCO World Heritage Register) tell us the duke's household consumed one ox, 6 quarters of beans (16*s* 8*d*) and 5 quarters of oats (£10 2*s* 8*d*). Having dispensed local justice, York left the Moot Hall early on 29 December. According to an eyewitness, on leaving the town of Wakefield (we are told York was heading to York), his household and baggage were ambushed by men loyal to the Earl of Northumberland. In the fighting, Richard Anson, MP for Hull, was killed; Sir Thomas Harrington was mortally wounded; his son was killed; and John Sclatter suffered 'great injuries and mutilations suffered in the wars of our noble father at Wakefield, where he lost his right hand and badly injured the other, so that he may neither clothe nor feed himself'.

After a short skirmish, York and his household was captured and taken back to the Moot Hall. The battlefield itself is somewhere under the City Fields development. The land here was owned by Lionel, 6th Baron Welles, an enemy of York since the Battle of Blore Heath, where he was made a prisoner by the Yorkists.

Early on 30 December, the Earl of Northumberland and Lord Clifford began killing their prisoners – possibly in Manor House Yard or the Bull Ring, where in 1460 the town's gallows stood. Executed in the Bull Ring were Sir Edward Bourchier, William Bonville, Sir James Strangeways, Richard Hansard and Geoffrey Southwarth. Their bodies were dumped in a mass grave outside what is now the cathedral. York was still alive. The Lancastrians 'proceed to trash' the surrounding countryside, driving cattle, pigs and other livestock to Pontefract. Sandal Castle was set on fire.

Some of the Yorkist high command escaped the carnage but were captured late that evening and taken to Pontefract. The prisoners were housed in St Richard's Friary. Early on 31 December 1460 Andrien Treslot murdered the Duke of York. Amongst the prisoners in the friary was the seventeen-year-old Earl of Rutland, who was executed by Lord Clifford. William Plumpton then executed the Earl of Salisbury and his son, Thomas. Also hacked

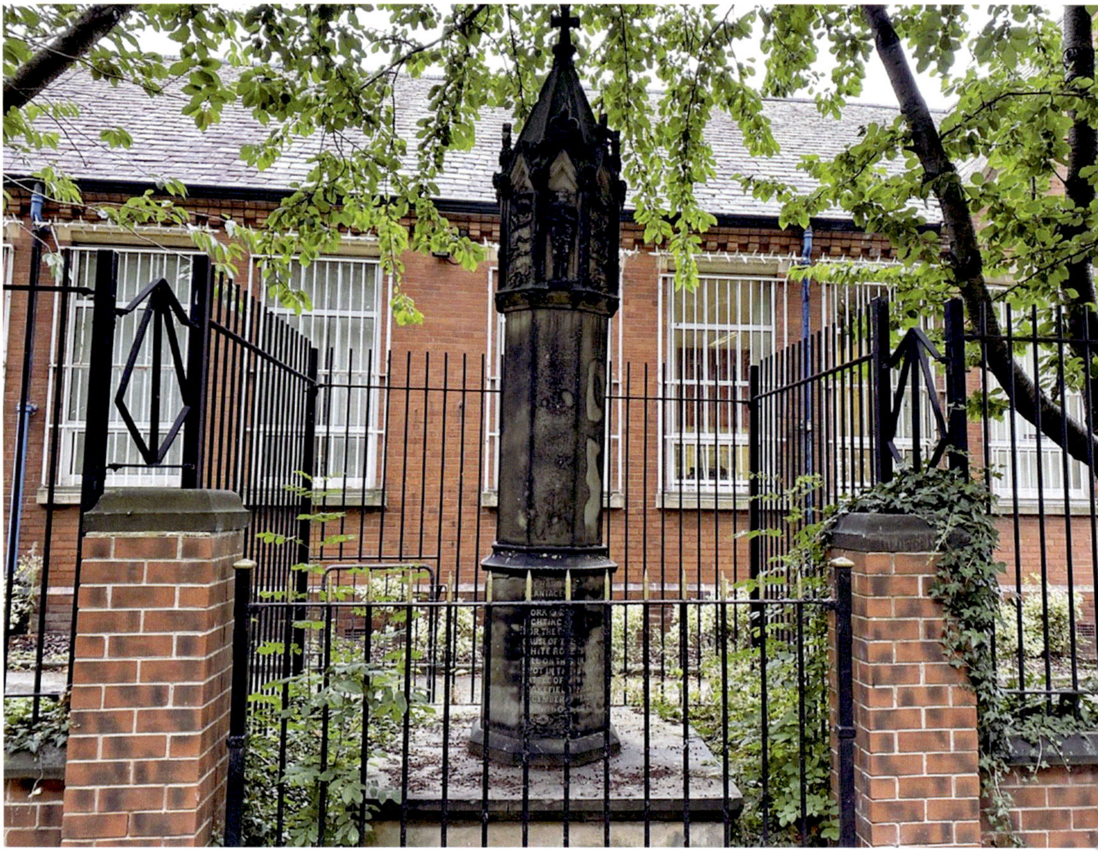

Erected at the end of the nineteenth century, reportedly on the spot where the Duke of York was killed in battle on 30 December 1460. Archive evidence shows the battle was fought on 29 December and the duke was murdered in Pontefract. The cross has nothing to do with the battle, and is a work of whimsy.

to death at Pontefract was Londoner John Harrowe. Parliament posthumously convicted Northumberland of murder in November 1461 – he and much of his household had been killed at Towton. The Earl of Salisbury's widow took legal action against those alive after Towton at the court of King's Bench, who found them guilty.

Sometime on 2 January, the Earl of Northumberland left Pontefract for Beverley, carrying with him the heads of York, Salisbury and Rutland. Their bodies were dumped in a grave at St Richard's Friary. Clifford threatened to kill the surviving members of Salisbury's household, but settled instead for physical violence and extortion.

The Battle of Wakefield marked a significant turning point in the code of chivalry. In previous conflicts the bodies of nobles had been respected, but this was not so at Wakefield. The mutilated cadavers of the Yorkist nobility became weapons in a brutal propaganda war. In a similar vein, being taken prisoner for ransom and treated as an honoured guest, that most chivalrous of virtues, was abandoned at Wakefield and instead people were executed. Richard's fate echoed that of his namesake son. His blood-soaked

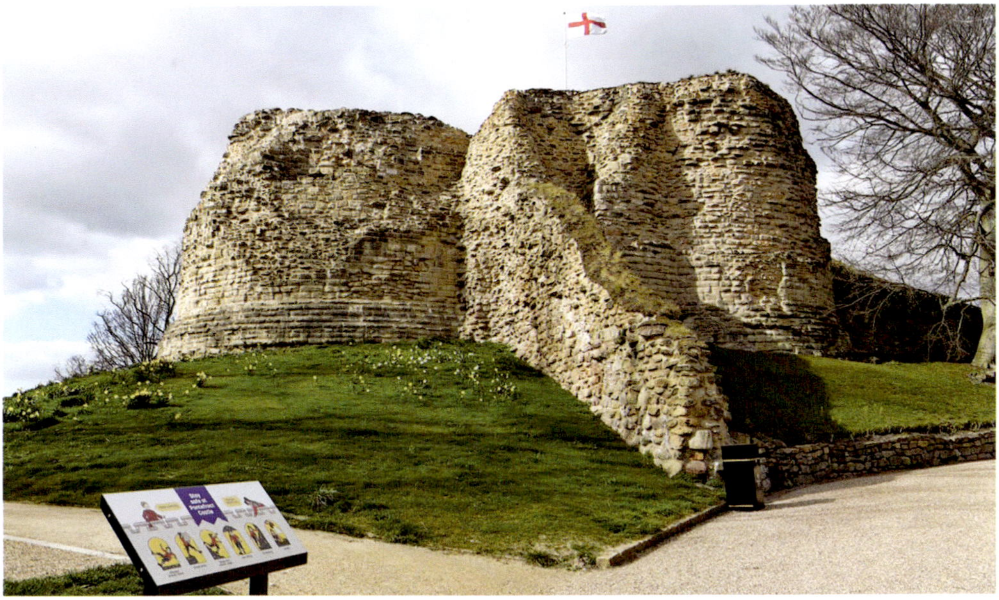

The ruins of Pontefract Castle. It was here at Pontefract where the Duke of York, his son the Earl of Rutland, the Earl of Salisbury and other high-ranking Yorkists were executed on 31 December 1460.

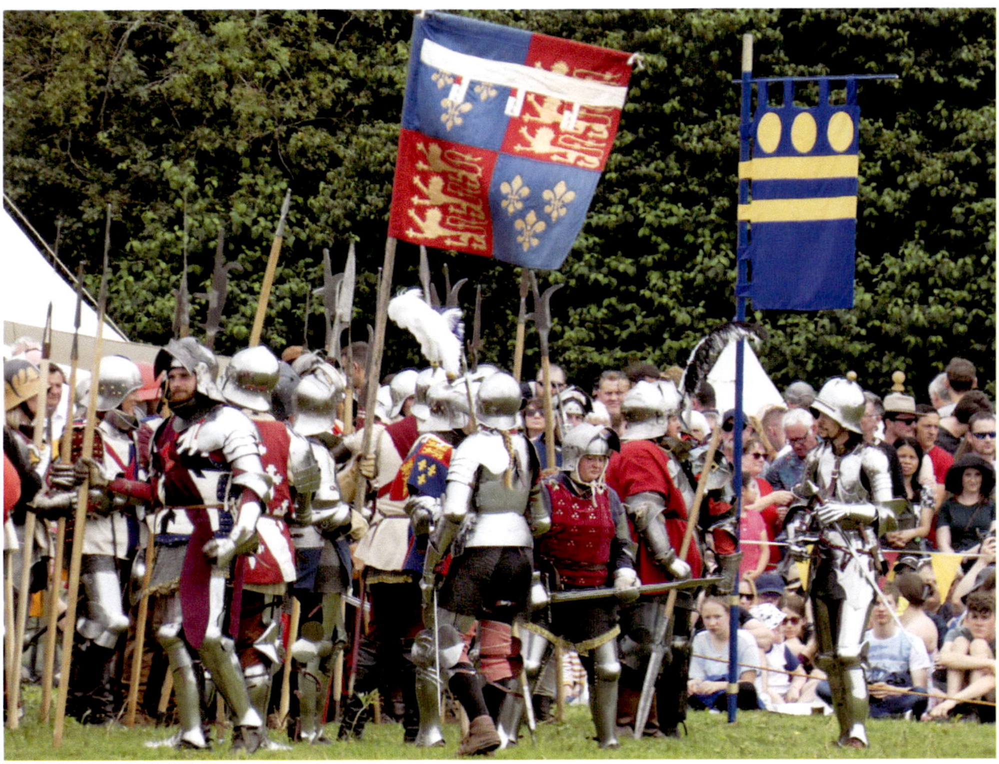

These re-enactors are dressed in armour identical to that worn at the Battle of Wakefield in 1460.

corpse was slung on a horse and carried to Pontefract for burial. His body was abused en route before being decapitated.

The brutality of the Lancastrians served to draw allies to Richard's son, Edward, who was now the legal heir to the throne. The defeat at Wakefield was reversed at Towton when Edward swept to victory and was named Edward VI.

We cannot say with certainty where the battle was fought. It was once believed that the battlefield was at Manygates, but this is not true, and the cross there does not mark the spot where the Duke of York was killed. In 1825, when digging out a field boundary dating from 1450–1500 somewhere near Potobello House, bones were discovered alongside a

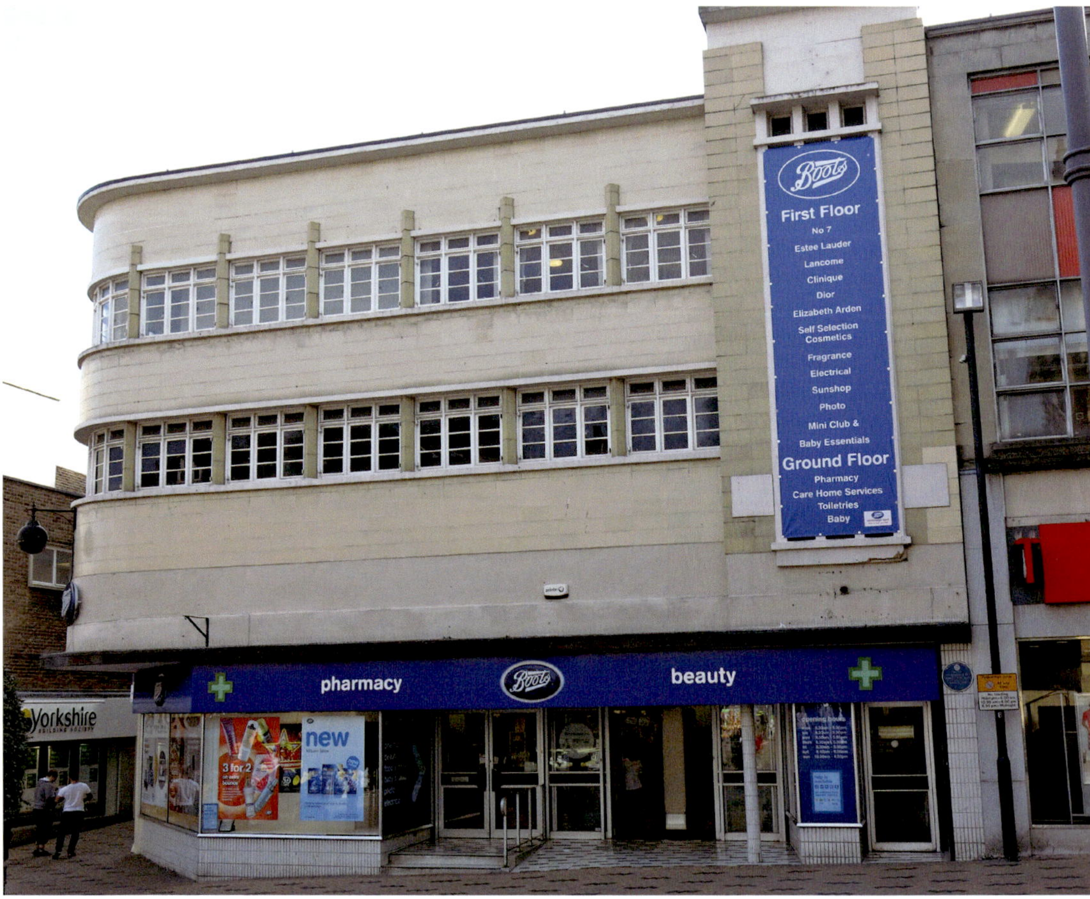

Boots the Chemist stands where in 1460 part of the medieval manor house of Wakefield stood. Mentioned in 1308 as the Earl's Hall (also known as the New Hall and the Wood Hall), it was a large and prestigious building, and grand enough and large enough to house the retinue of Earl Warenne, then lord of the manor. Enlarged and modernised, by 1460 this was the largest and grandest house in Wakefield, supplanting the old and outdated castle at Sandal. In 1539 the great hall became the Moot Hall, the courthouse for the manor of Wakefield. The last vestiges of the manor were torn down in the 1950s.

sword. At the time the bones were believed to be human remains and the sword was thought to be an infantry or bowman's sidearm or hanger. They were seen as evidence that this was the battlefield site, but that is not necessarily the case. For one, the bones no longer exist for us to determine whether they were actually human. The sword was only believed to be from the battle because it was found on what had already been assumed to be the battlefield site, but one does not prove the other. As with all battlefield finds, caution should be exercised in associating the sword with the battle in the absence of corroborative archaeological evidence, especially as the find spot is totally unknown. The supposed 'facts' of the battle are actually assumptions that have been made since the 1860s and then blindly repeated.

The battlefield was somewhere in Stanley. Accounts from the manor of Wakefield tell us that cloth bandages were brought from Stanley to dress the wounds of the injured. Logic tells us that if you need bandages, you get them from as close as possible to the wounded – ergo, Stanley. The earliest account of the battle tells us the duke was going north from Wakefield to York. This account, along with eyewitnesses to the battle and the manor of Wakefield records all point to the battle being north of Wakefield, somewhere in Stanley. It is called the Battle of Wakefield because this is where the battle ended and the duke was killed, not because this is where the battle was.

As could be easily understood, the Battle of Wakefield became a key piece of propaganda to 'prop up' the ailing regime of Henry VIII (r. 1509–47). His unpopular marriage to Anne Boleyn, the break with the papacy and consequential religious changes, the Pilgrimage of Grace in 1536–37 (a direct response to Henry's break with the Church) and the enclosure of common land that sparked rioting in 1535 all marked a rising tide of tensions towards Henry, as he increasingly became a despotic tyrant. The abortive military coup known as the Wakefield Plot of March 1541 was followed by a massive – and armed – royal progress to the north that summer, which we shall discuss later. Thus, in the aftermath of these events it is hardly surprising that we see print culture promoting the Tudor – and therefore Lancastrian – side of history, reminding the country as a whole of the fate of those who opposed the Crown.

Therefore, Richard, Duke of York had to be painted to be a usurper of the Lancastrian throne to enhance the current regime and its links to the house of Lancaster. The more Richard's reputation was blackened, as with that of his son Richard III (r. 1452–85), and the more gratuitous the details of his death, the better. Richard's reputation, like that of his sons, became part of the Tudor misinformation campaign by their propagandist-in-chief, Shakespeare. Indeed, chronicles by Hall, Stowe, Renin, Benet and Polydor Virgil to name a few, as well as Shakespeare's rendering and the uncritical examination of the written sources from the Tudor court, have enabled a whole fictitious narrative to be created of the battle that lingers to the current day. We have to look behind the later political spin to establish some modicum of reality.

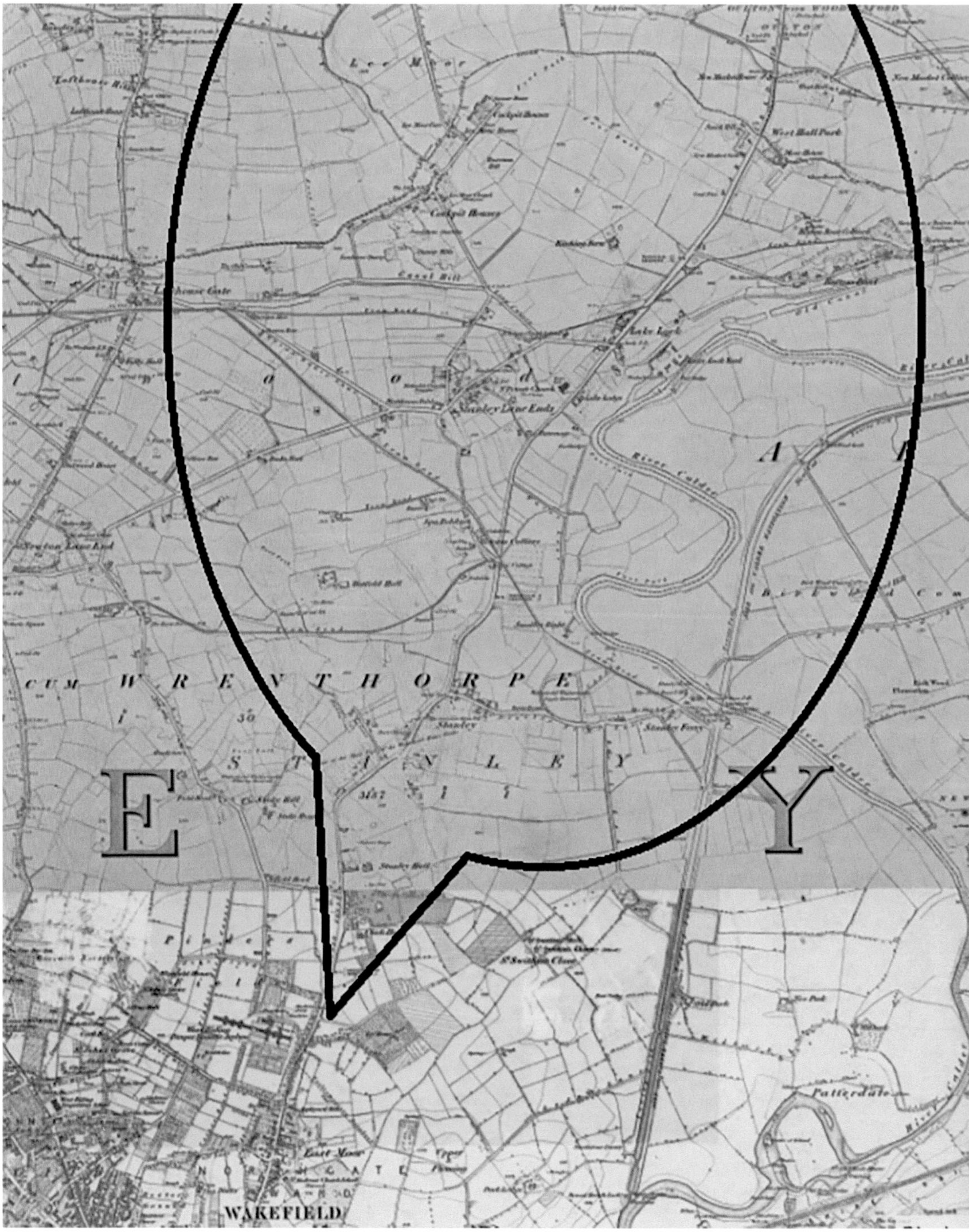

Sketch map showing the probable battle site of the Battle of Wakefield.

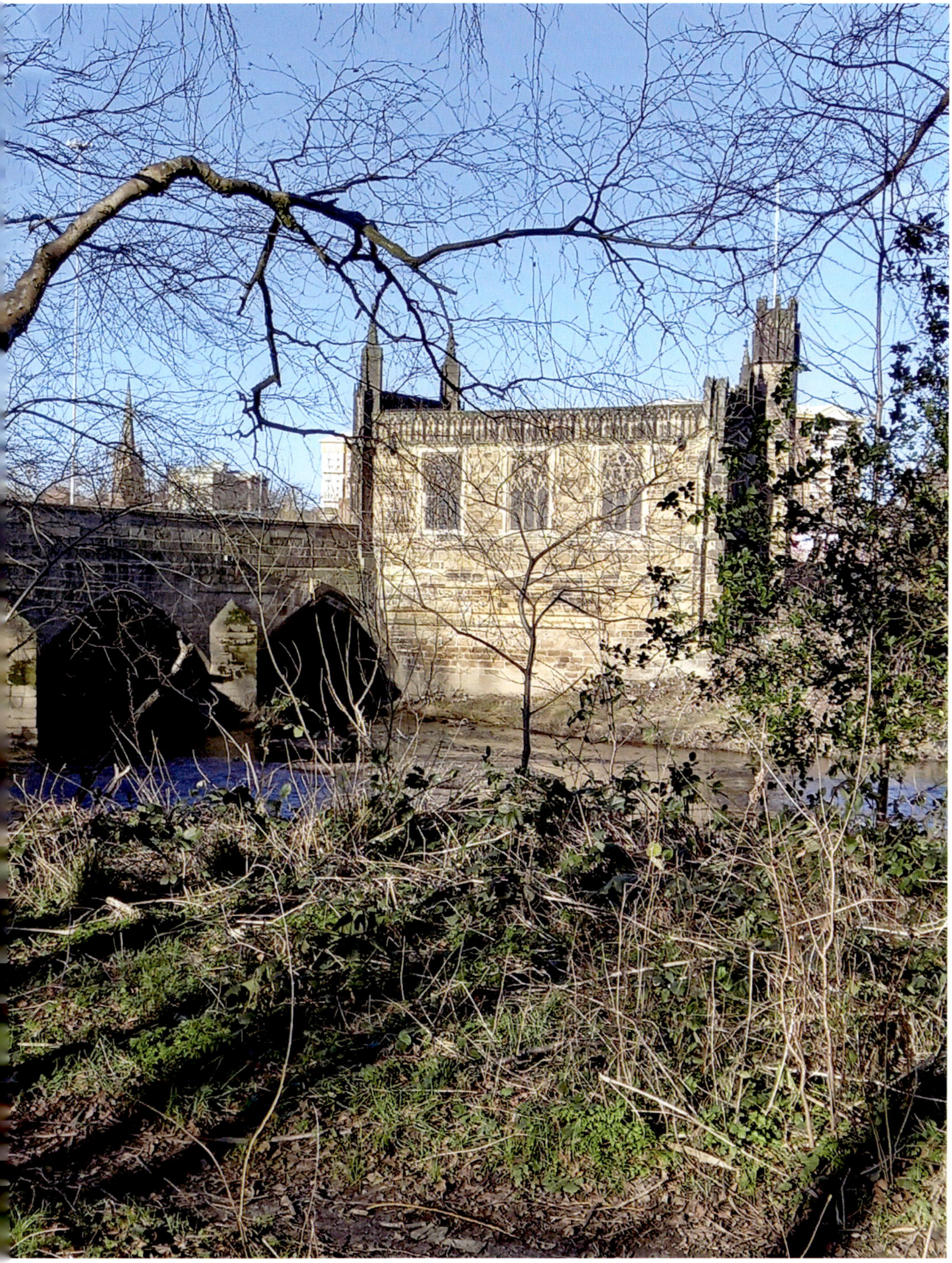

Wakefield bridge and chantry chapel. Myth says this is where the Earl of Rutland was killed, but he was actually murdered in Pontefract.

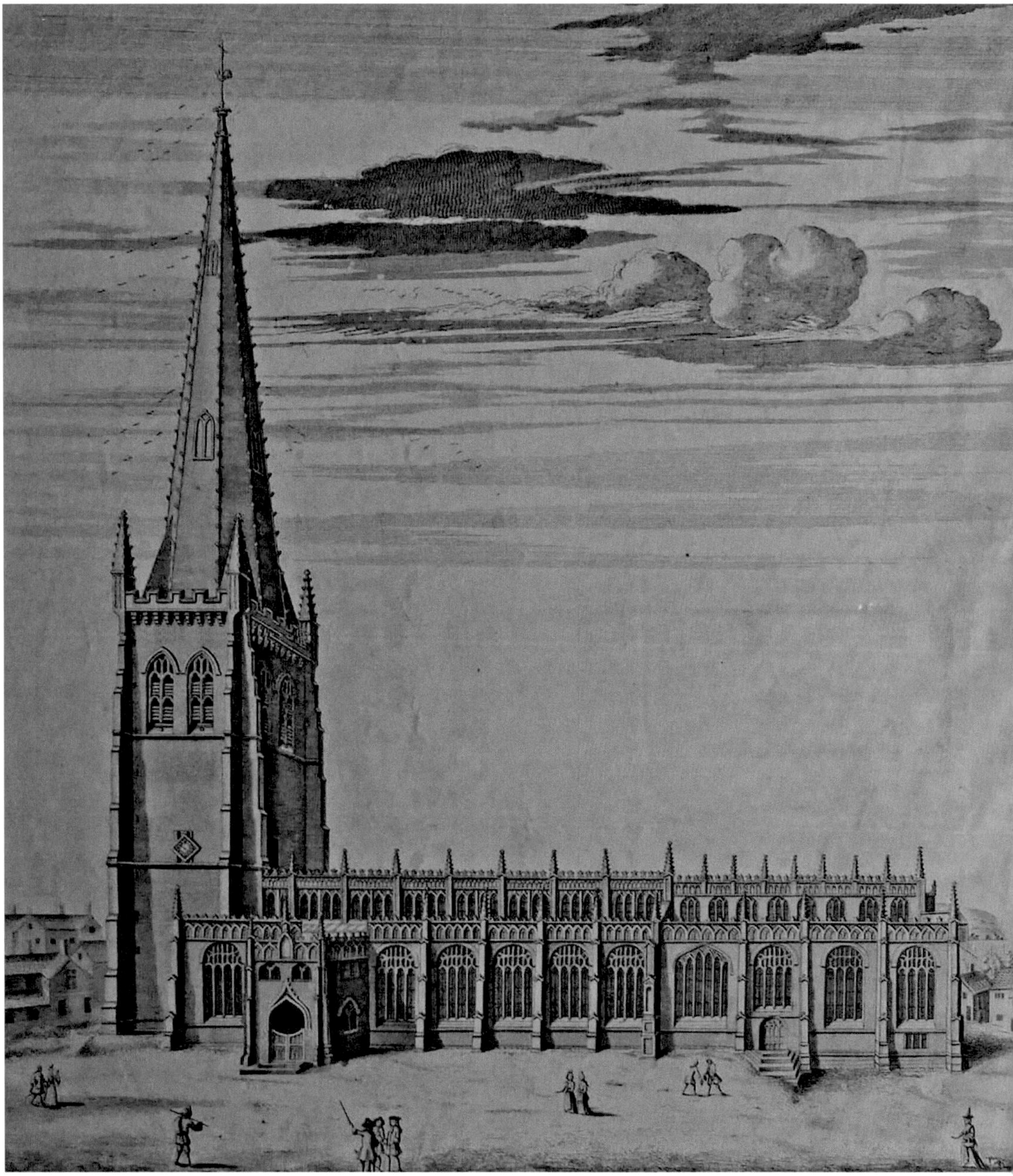

Wakefield Parish Church of All Saints, drawn *c.* 1690. The two right-hand windows of the church are the windows of the now destroyed Richard III Chapel, built by Sir Thomas Pilkington in the 1470s. No trace of the chantry exists. It was suppressed during the reign of Edward IV and destroyed in the 1890s, with the eastern extension to the church completed 1903–05. No Mass has been said for the soul of the king since 1549.

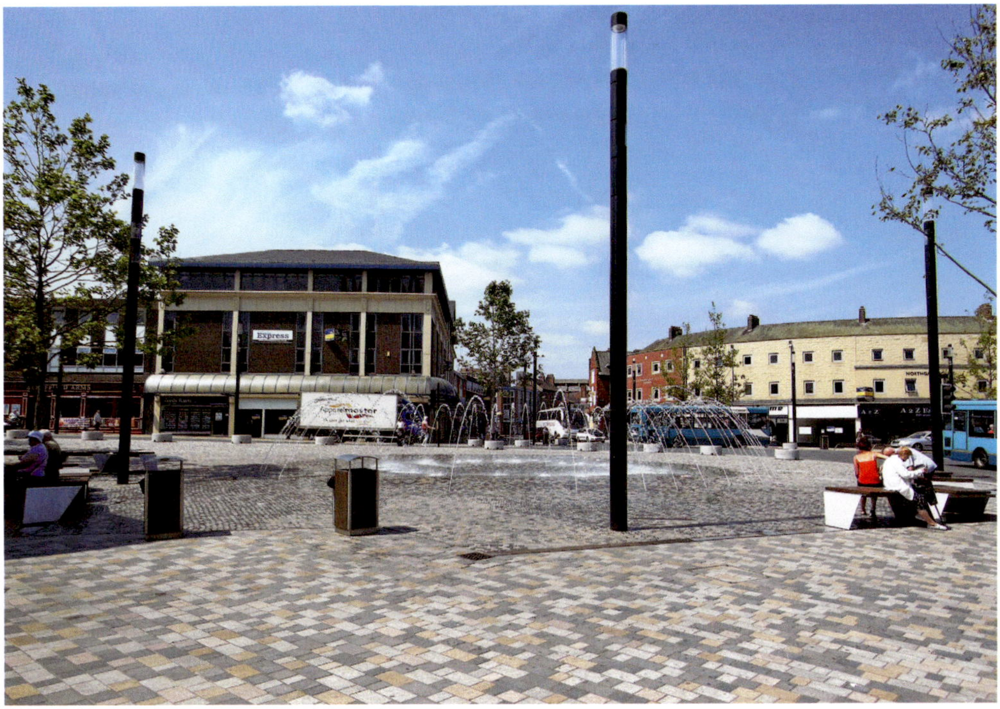

Where fountains play in 2025 was the site of the town's gallows in 1460. Known as 'Bitch Hill', it was here that followers of Richard, Duke of York were murdered on 30 December 1460, having been captured in combat the day before.

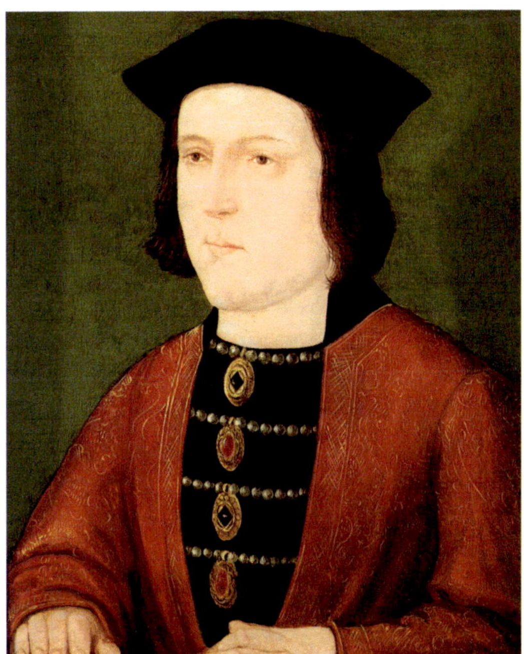

Following the death of Richard, Duke of York at Pontefract, his son Edward became king. The Act of Accord in October 1460 made the Duke of York and his heirs heirs to the throne of England and not the son of Henry VI. With the duke's death, Edward was heir to the throne and won the crown at the Battle of Towton. Edward spent a night in Wakefield in 1471 during his campaign to retake the crown following the Readeption of Henry VI.

3. Tudor Rebellions

With the demise of Richard III, the youngest son of Richard, 3rd Duke of York, at the Battle of Bosworth in 1485, an obscure Welshman named Henry Tudor became monarch as Henry VII (r. 1485–1509). This heralded the short-lived and ultimately unsuccessful Tudor dynasty, which, like the previous Plantagenet era, was defined by bloodshed and turbulence. Henry VII's reign alone saw the Simnel Rebellion of 1486–87, the Yorkshire Rebellion of 1489 and the Warbeck Rebellion of 1497. The Wars of the Roses were not yet over.

To defend Britanny, an English ally against France, Henry VII levied £100,000 in new taxes, which was to be collected by Henry Percy, Earl of Northumberland. In the wake of famine and heavy taxation the previous year to pay for war with Scotland, in April 1489 the people of Yorkshire rose in revolt. Percy was murdered and in response Henry sent a large army of 8,000 to the north, led by Thomas, Earl of Surrey. The rebels dispersed and the rebel leader, John à Chambre, was hanged for treason and was succeeded by Sir John Egremont (an illegitimate member of the house of Percy) as leader. Following defeat, he fled to the court of Margaret of Burgundy (daughter of Richard, 3rd Duke of York). The results of this rebellion led the rebels to receive a royal pardon, and no further taxes were collected; thus, Henry was unable to raise enough money to defend Brittany. He also became aware of the lawless nature of the north of England, which had been loyal to Richard III, who had spent more time in the north than any previous King of England.

Henry VII was succeeded by his son, Henry VIII (r. 1509–47), who through breaking with the papacy cascaded the country into chaos once more. There were rebellions against his rule and that of his daughter Elizabeth (r. 1558–1603), the most important being the Pilgrimage of Grace, the aborted Wakefield Rebellion of 1541 (as much a religious protest as one about taxation) and the Rising of the North in 1569.

The events in England were no different to tensions in Europe at the time. The Continent was divided between Catholics on one side and a range of differing Protestant beliefs – Lutherans, Presbyterians, Puritans, Anabaptists, Unitarians and Calvinists to name a few – that tore Europe apart for almost 150 years. These wars of religion shaped national identity.

News of Henry VIII replacing the pope as head of the newly established Church of England in 1531 sparked tension. What happened next was not just about religion, but also about rich landowners enclosing common land for sheep and Henry VIII raising new taxes to fight Catholic Europe. Riots against enclosure broke out in 1532 in Rothwell, Wakefield and Halifax. In September 1535 anger boiled over against Cromwell and other advisors of the king, as well as against new taxes. Henry sent the Duke of Norfolk to the north and rebellion was nipped in the bud in Wakefield and Halifax. It surprised no one –

other than the king – that in October 1536 simmering tensions broke out into nascent civil war with the Pilgrimage of Grace.

The uprising, after which Wakefield men were executed for taking arms against the king, was motivated by the king's religious changes, the Dissolution of the Monasteries and tax impositions. A number of local economic complaints were also added to the list of grievances.

Wakefield was at the forefront of what happened. On 12 October it was reported by Sir Richard Tempest, the steward of the manor, that the people of the town were in rebellious mood and that 'the king's commissioners [probably those appointed to assess the latest instalment of the 1534 royal subsidy], did not dare sit in the town'. Later that month the

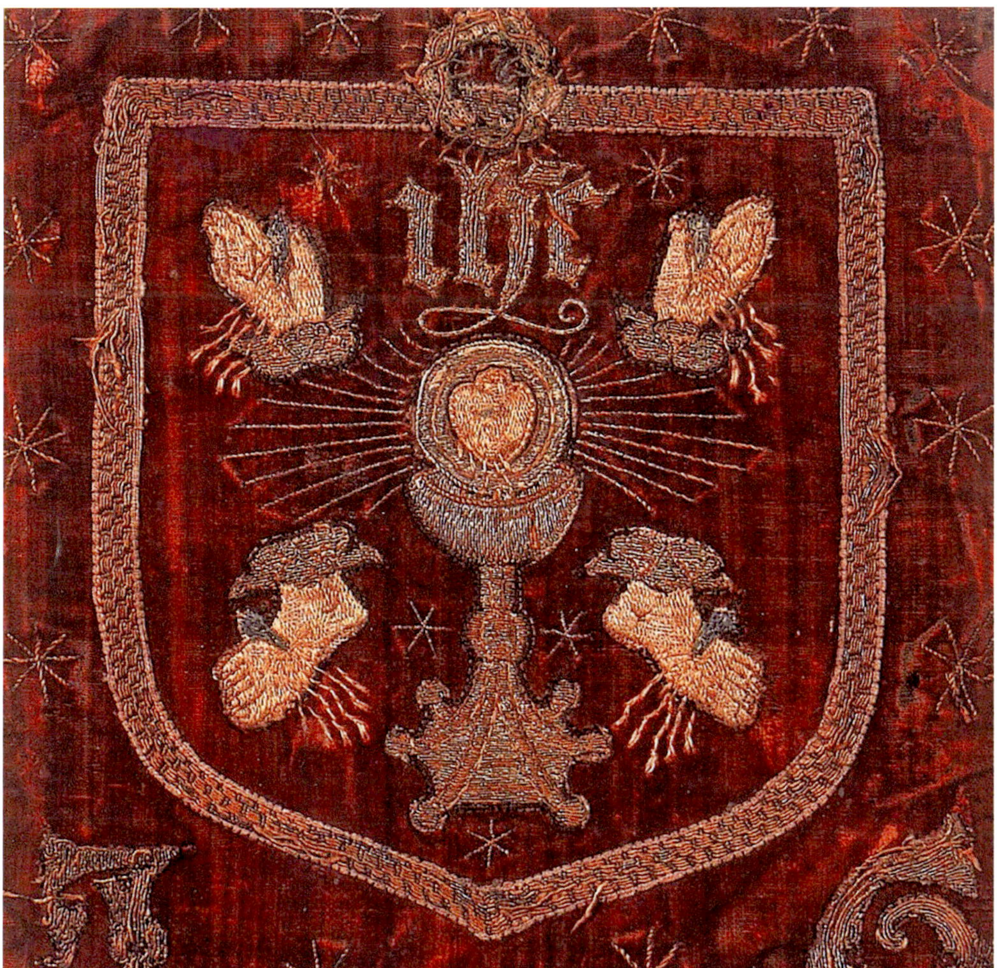

The Pilgrimage of Grace (1536) was one of the most serious rebellions against Henry VIII and his religious policies. The birth of the Anglican church was marked in violence, martyrdom and bloodshed. This banner, showing the five wounds of Christ, was the symbol of the pilgrimage.

West Riding towns responded eagerly to a call from the priest Thomas Maunsell to rebel against the king's policies over taxation, enclosure and religious changes, not his rule. Over 30,000 assembled at Pontefract Castle, which was quickly captured. According to Maunsell, 10,000 men were raised in Wakefield and drew leadership from the abbot of the Cluniac monastery in Pontefract, the Knights Hospitallers at Newland, as well as the prior at St Oswald's Priory at Nostell.

The men from Wakefield marched to Doncaster to face down the King's army. Sir Richard Tempest, the steward of the manor of Wakefield, initially assembled loyalists at the Moot Hall who ordered the town to be defended against the rebellious army on 15 October. He and his sons, realising that if they opposed the pilgrims they would be murdered, defected to join the rebellion. So strong was local opposition to Henry VIII that the steward of Sandal Castle, Thomas Gryce, opened the gates and let the pilgrims take the castle, its stores of food and arsenal of weapons. With two castles, support of local gentry families and monastic foundations, the success of the rebellion seemed assured.

The rebellion's leaders hoped that the kings of Scotland and France would send 40,000 men to their aid. In this they were naïve. One of the demands made to the king was that Wakefield should have the right to send two MPs to London and that enclosure of common land and wasteland should end. None of these demands were met, and Wakefield only gained an MP in 1831. Faced with overwhelming opposition, and fearing invasion, the king agreed to pardon all those involved in November 1536: with an army of less than 8,000 he had no choice but to negotiate or face the prospect of all out civil war. When rebellion broke out again in spring 1537, primarily Henry's fault for not keeping his terms of the truce. His retribution was swift and merciless: 216 men were executed amongst which were several lords and knights, seven abbots, thirty-eight monks and sixteen parish priests. Sir Richard Tempest was gaoled, where he died in August 1539; his son Nicholas who had raised Halifax for the Pilgrimage, was executed at Tyburn in July 1537.

The Wakefield Plot

After the 1537 rebellion, causes of discontent continued to increase in the north as the larger monastic houses were dissolved. If anything, the Pilgrimage hardened Henry's attitudes. Religious changes continued, notably the requirement that churches should have a Bible in English, which was unpopular and had to be enforced by Cranmer. In 1539 Henry dissolved all the monasteries that had survived the cull of 1536. The monastic houses were primarily vast farming estates that controlled the economic base of Yorkshire; the trade in wool, woollen cloth and iron production was almost totally controlled by the monasteries. By 1540 monasteries were being dismantled at a rate of fifty a month. Closing the monasteries resulted in the dislocation of the woollen trade and vast swathes of land passing to the Crown. The long-established moral economy was swept away almost overnight by the King. Thus, we can easily see that the Dissolution had both an emotional and economic aspect, given the attachment to traditional religion demonstrated in the Pilgrimage of Grace. The monasteries had dominated the woollen trade, so the Dissolution not only changed the faith of the nation, it destroyed the economic basis of the north. Indeed, Robert Aske had noted this as a primary cause of the earlier rebellion.

Compounding the Dissolution, Henry's break with Rome left England isolated and vulnerable to invasion from Catholic Europe. So seriously had Henry taken that threat that he'd initiated a massive programme of coastal defensive works. However, it had been done so poorly and hastily that by 1541 many were falling down. Taxes rose to pay for the works, further impoverishing an already economically depressed area. Ambassador Chapuys from the Holy Roman Emperor, tells us the king had seized the rentals from northern abbeys like Jervaulx and Fountains and diverted it to London, financially ruining many merchants in the north to fund these works.

The spark for the rebellion appears to have been James V of Scotland levying troops to invade the north of England with prompting from Francis I of France. Already a tinder box of discontent, Yorkshire needed little prompting to rise up – the vicar of Wakefield, Edward Eland, had been in trouble in 1538 for spreading seditious songs against Thomas Cromwell. Led by the Neville family of Chevet and other local gentry families, the plotters planned to attend Pontefract Fair on 10 April 1541 and canvass the town for support (then the de facto capital of the West Riding). Once they had rallied those gathered at the fair to their cause, the plotters were to 'denounce and declare against the King's bad government and tyranny, and attack and slay all those who should rise in defence of the common-wealth'.

As in 1536–37, the plotters' goal was to take possession of Pontefract Castle, kill Robert Holgate and wait for military aid from Scotland. Considered to be a protégé of Thomas Cromwell, Holgate was appointed president of the Council in the North in 1538, a post he held for eleven years. He lived in the house of the former abbot of St Mary's Abbey in York, which has survived as King's Manor. Holgate, like Cromwell, was hated for his influence over the king and for his part in the break with Rome. We forget that people's faith cannot be simply changed by the king's whim. The Church of England was born amidst bloodshed, murder, mayhem and almost all-out civil war.

The conspirators planned to gather a military force at Pontefract, as had occurred with huge success in 1536. Sandal Castle was also a target to secure the road from London. After Henry's deceit in 1536, a rebel army was unlikely to be persuaded to disperse in return for promises from the ling. Henry could no longer be called a mild and just man deceived by 'wicked advisors' as the 1536 plotters claimed. He was a cold, ruthless tyrant.

The scene was set for a showdown. Yet, the plotters were betrayed. If we leave out those released after questioning, twenty-six people were arrested – seventeen lay persons and nineteen priests. Of these, fifteen were executed, including Sir John Neville of Chevet, William Leigh of Leeds (he had rebelled against Henry previously and was clearly a wanted man) and the following from Wakefield: wool merchant Thomas Tattersall; Gilbert Thornton; James Diamond, who had assisted some of the participants in the Pilgrimage of Grace to flee to Scotland or France; Willaim Swynden, a chantry priest at Wakefield Parish Church; John Grice, a priest serving Sandal Parish Church; and Robert Box of Box Hall, near Clarke Hall. Others involved were Oswald Grice, a chantry priest at the parish church, and William Cookson.

With his kingship threatened again, Henry set off north with a retinue of 5,000 men at arms and his court in a show of pomp and triumph to cower the populace with 'shock and awe'. Ambassador Chapuys even went as far as to suggest that the plot was far more

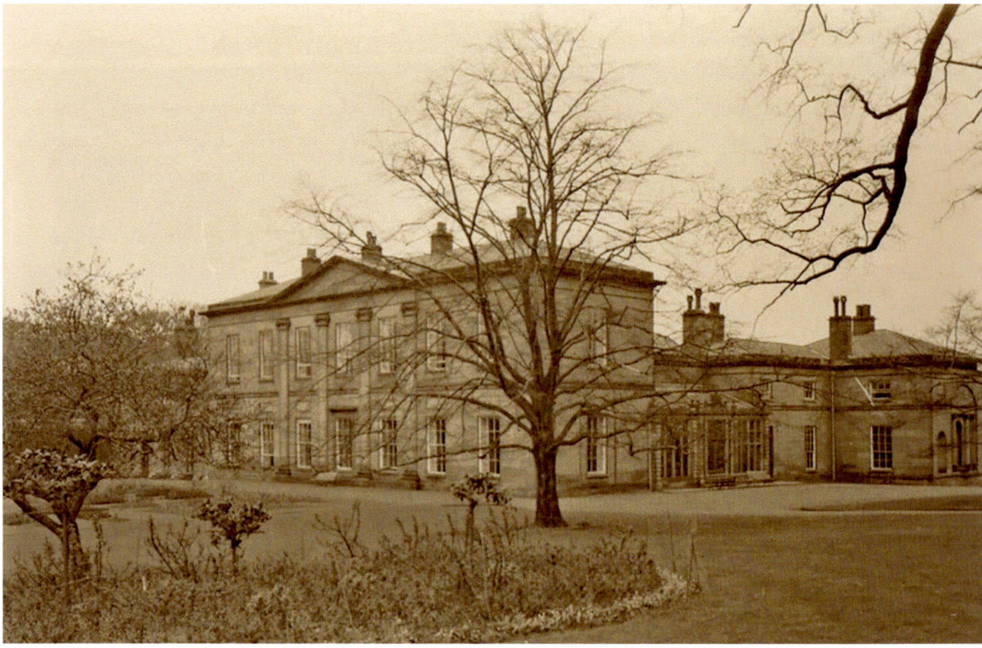

Despite its Palladian appearance, Chevet Hall was a late medieval house hidden behind a stone façade. The house was built in 1529 by the Nevile family and was bought in 1765 by Sir Lionel Pilkington, 5th Baronet, and passed down through the Pilkington family. In 1954 the estate was acquired as a country park by Wakefield Council, who demolished the hall in the 1960s. It was here that the Wakefield Plot was masterminded.

dangerous than that of 1536/37. Hence, Henry embarked on one of the largest – if not *the* largest – royal progresses of the era. The whole entourage with the king was larger than the population of both Wakefield and Pontefract at the time.

Fearing trouble, rather than head through the West Riding Henry changed his plans and headed to Pontefract via Hessle in the East Riding – a symbolic act to reclaim Pontefract Castle for the Crown after its involvement in the 1356, 1537 and 1541 plots. The king spent a week at Pontefract before heading to York. So successful was Henry's 'shock and awe' that no major rebellion in the north occurred for a generation. The Wakefield Plot was quickly shuffled out of history.

Henry's resulting progress bound the northern elites to the king through a succession of choreographed supplications from the northern gentry and yeomen; the rituals of submission and forgiveness, repeated at place after place, bound the ruling elites firmly to the king. Despite serious fears that the progress might meet with trouble in the north, it succeeded in pacifying the region.

As historian C. J. Sansom has eloquently argued, the Wakefield Plot, an attempted military coup, presented a real and present danger to Henry VIII. It was well planned, involved unprecedented inter-class collaboration and had aid from the Scots, with whom the conspirators seem to have had links, who envisaged a bloody conflict to overthrow the 'tyrant' Henry. The plot demonstrates that the Reformation was hated and very slow to gain ground outside elite circles. The change from Catholic to Protestant faith was not an overnight event, regardless of how Henry understood it to be. It was a generational-long transition.

The Northern Rebellion

This shift in national faith to Protestantism is best reflected in the events that took place in the last months of 1569, when the earls of Northumberland and Westmorland rebelled against the queen in an attempt to preserve Catholicism.

Surveyed in 1566 by the Crown, Sandal Castle was in a fairly dilapidated condition – roofs were missing, so were floors. The queen ordered the castle to be repaired as it occupied a strategic location in the north. Overseeing the work was Edward Carey, the grandson of the 'other Boleyn girl', Mary. The establishment of the Elizabethan settlement alienated those who favoured the old religion, and their disaffection increased as growing numbers were arrested and imprisoned for religious nonconformity. This disaffection was spurred by the arrival in England of Mary, Queen of Scots, in 1568, and many sought to place her on the throne and oust Elizabeth to restore Catholicism. Rebellion broke out in May 1569.

Unlike 1541, this time rather fighting the state, men from Wakefield took up arms for Queen Elizabeth. Henry Cecil noted: 'The Queen understands many ways that both in Lincolnshire, in Nottinghamshire, and about Doncaster and Wakefield, there are to be had great numbers of able men to serve, so as they had armour and weapons.'

The rebellion of 1569 was part of a European-wide war of religion which was tearing the Continent apart. Edward Carey hastily raised a defence force at Sandal, aided by Sir Thoms Gargrave, the vice president of the Council of the North. Under the 1538 Militia Act Thomas Waterton of Walton was to find two corselets, two pikes, two plate coats, a bow with arrows, a musket and a helmet; John Saville of Wakefield was to provide a corselet, musket, helmet and bow with arrows; Hugh Saville of Wrenthorpe, Robert Bradford of Clarke Hall, Leonard Bate of Lupset and Henry Grice of Sandal were to each provide a corselet, musket, pike and helmet along with a box and arrows; Robert Kaye of Wakefield, Walter Calverley of Stanley, Ralph Blacker of Crigglestone, Robert Hobson of Stanley, John Bunny of Wakefield and others were to provide a coat of mail, a long bow and arrows, and a bill. Sir Edward Carey established himself at Sandal, the castle housing 300 corselets with helmets for pikemen and 100 bows. Sandal Castle 'was armed about with iron gonnes', which were presumably small calibre artillery pieces, likely to be the breach loaders mentioned in a survey of 1531. Fighting took place outside Durham, and the rebellion was supressed by the start of 1571.

The wars of religion, which shattered France and tore apart Europe, were used by the Tudor state to spin a story of nationhood against adversity: the state was defined as Protestant, as opposed to European Catholicism. 'Englishness' was defined as oppositional to Catholicism, anti-French and increasingly anti-European. In creating this new identity, the state coerced the populus to convert to Protestantism through legislation and patronage for the wealthiest in society, imposed top down and often against the will of the people – from lord to commoner by the Crown in an act of royal power. Royal power was at the heart of what happened next after Elizabeth's death.

4. The English Civil War

War over religion in Europe had ended briefly with the Edict of Nantes in 1598. Yet, peace did not last. The assassination of Henry IV of France in 1610 led to a European-wide conflict: the thirty years' war (1618–48). England, Scotland and Ireland were sucked into this conflict, which British history refers to as the Civil War or the War of Three Kingdoms. The English Civil War is a generic term for a series of conflicts between Royalists and Parliamentarians in England and Wales from 1639 to 1653. The end of the First Civil War, in 1646, left a partial power vacuum in which any combination of the three English factions – Royalists, Independents (largely Puritans) of the New Model Army ('the Army') and Presbyterians of the English Parliament (who sought to remodel the Church of England in removing bishops and episcopal succession) – as well as the Scottish Parliament allied with the Scottish Presbyterians (the 'Kirk'), could prove strong enough to dominate the rest. From 1646 to 1648 the tensions between the Army and Parliament – on religious and political grounds – widened day by day. Until, finally, the Presbyterian faction, combined with the Scots and the remaining Royalists, felt itself strong enough to begin a Second Civil War (1648–49) which resulted in the execution of Charles I (r. 1603–49). With the execution of the king, Oliver Cromwell led the country as Lord Protector (in power 1649–58). A third civil war broke out in 1649–51, culminating in the battles of Dunbar and Worcester, securing Cromwell's power.

As with almost every town and village in the country, the English Civil war greatly affected Wakefield. Sandal Castle was besieged and demolished and the town was attacked in a little-known battle. The taking of the town by the Parliamentary army in May 1643 was surely one of the strangest encounters of the Civil War.

Why was the area important? The clothing districts of the West Riding were strategically important to both sides in the conflict for two reasons: firstly, the towns had money – always useful for paying soldiers – and the cloth produced here clothed both soldiers of the king and Parliament; secondly, for Parliament, the area was one of the key recruiting areas. The north had a long history of opposition to the Crown – primarily against what was considered to be unjust taxation – and was home to growing communities of religious Dissenters, who were opposed to Church and king on theological and political grounds. By 1662, over 155 Dissenter congregations existed in Yorkshire, many of which were founded by soldiers who fought for Parliament: Captain Joseph Poole was a founding member of a congregation in Wakefield; Colonel Phillip Twistleton founded his own congregation in Drax; Captain Rhodes of Houghton, near Barnsley, founded a chapel at Great Houghton and another at Bullhouse. It was from these Presbyterian and Puritan communities that Parliament drew its northern supporters. For example, on 2 February 1643 Fairfax issued an appeal to all mayors, alderman, bailiffs and magistrates to rally to Parliament 'to defend the protestant religion' from the Royalist army 'and common enemies of the peace'. It was a war as much about religion as politics. We remember, in the context of the thirty years' war in Europe and the recent wars of religion in France – the surrender of the Huguenots in 1628 bringing to an end almost 100 years of conflict – religion, identity and self-determination were overriding themes of the epoch.

In England, the conflict between Protestant and what was seen as an increasingly Roman Catholic Church of England would put an end to Protestantism and, moreover, lead to an authoritarian regime like Louis XII had started to impose in France supported by Cardinal Richelieu. The wars of religion in France, beginning *c.* 1560, and the breaking out of civil war on religious lines in 1608 across Germany, lead to what became the most destructive war in Europe, with perhaps as many as 8 million being killed or dying from starvation and famine. Wakefield, like country as a whole, was not immune to religious tension, nor the events taking place in France, the Netherlands, Spain, Italy and what is now Germany.

The Battle of Wakefield

Now to return to the events of 1643. On 25 March, Bradford was held by the Parliamentarian forces led by Colonel Lambert and a vastly outnumbered and ill-trained 'citizens militia' beat off the Royalist attack. Five days later, another clash occurred at Seacroft Moor and the Parliamentarian forces, led by Thomas Fairfax, were roundly defeated. The Royalist commander, the Marquess of Newcastle, believed he could now lead his 10,000-strong army to 'liberate' the West Riding from Parliament. Consequently, General Lord George Goring and approximately 4,000 men were sent to Wakefield to hold the town.

Tension was high as Leeds was held by Fairfax. Around 800 Parliamentarians had been taken prisoner after being defeated at Seacroft Moor, and Fairfax plotted the capture of Wakefield to take prisoners of his own to exchange for his men. He marched his force from Leeds and split it into two columns to attack the town from different directions.

Around 2 a.m. on 21 May, Parliamentarian commanders Sir Henry Foullis and William Fairfax arrived at Stanley. Their troops overcame a picket from Goring's cavalry who had attempted to block Aberford Road with a barricade near Clarke Hall. Royalist dragoons (mounted soldiers) and musketeers opened fire from behind hedges and walls. The hedges provided a sufficient barrier against the attackers, so the barricade became the focus of the fighting.

After around two hours of fighting, as the dawn sun was starting to lighten the dark sky, Fairfax broke through into Wakefield. On news of the Parliamentarian attack, Goring, who had been in bed suffering from either illness or a hangover, was woken by a desperate messenger who had ridden 'hell for leather' from Clarke Hall to Heath Old Hall, home of Sir George Saville. Goring rose and led a counterattack in his nightshirt, sending out roughly 800 infantry and a squadron of cavalry to defend the town.

The second line of Royalist defences, close to where St Faith's Church once stood, were overcome by 6 a.m. following a charge by the Parliamentarian cavalry. Despite being vastly outnumbered, Sir Thomas Fairfax ordered Foullis and his brother, Sir William Fairfax, to lead the cavalry and a few companies of infantry to Northgate whilst he headed along Aberford Road with the bulk of the cavalry and remaining infantry, through Eastmoor to Warrengate. The narrow bridge over the Skitterick Beck had been destroyed

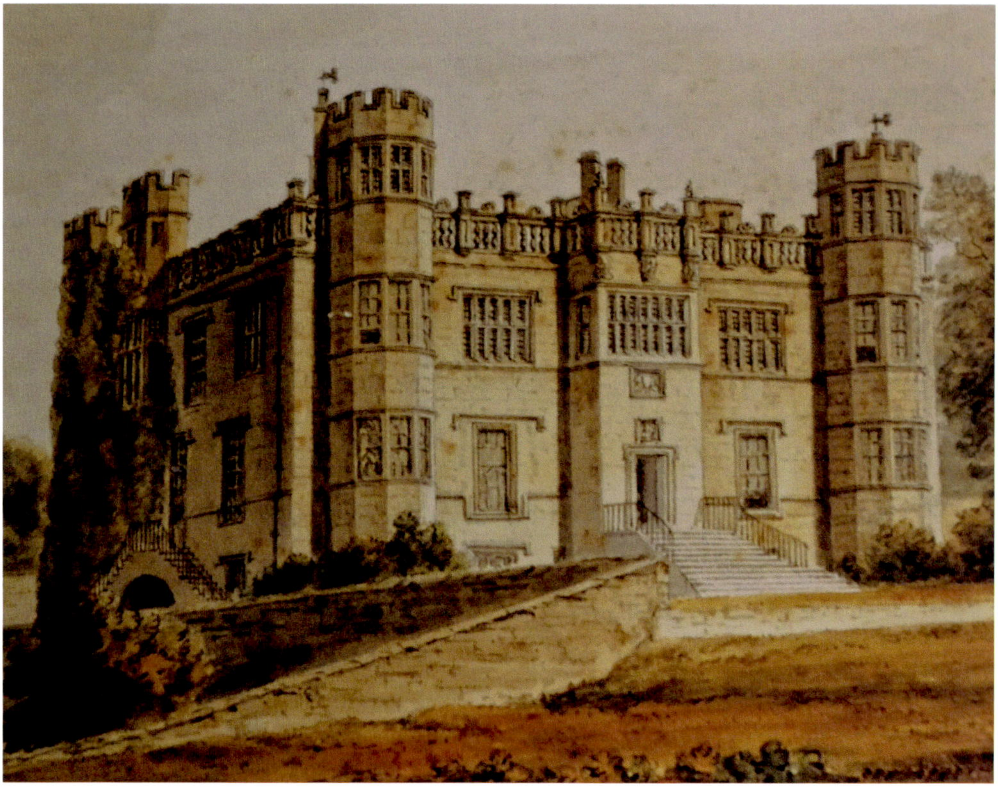

Heath Old Hall, headquarters of Lord Gorring. The house was, according to documents in the National Archives at Kew, built by the Saville family. It is described in a survey of 1607 as 'the new house of George Saville'. It was he who also built the innovative, but not unique, water tower. Saville was the son of the founder of Wakefield Grammar School. For obscure reasons, the house and water tower are ascribed by local legend to be the property of Dame Mary Bolles.

by the Royalists, who had barricaded Wrengate Head, hoping that the hedges and garden walls of the town would offer sufficient defence. After an hour fighting, Fairfax's men took the barricade and turned the royalist artillery against the town. Fairfax sought to exploit the situation, leaving his infantry in the command of George Gifford with orders to advance behind as quickly as possible. Dragging the captured artillery with them, Fairfax, at the head of his cavalry, charged headlong into the town along Warrengate.

Capturing the churchyard, his dismounted dragoons quickly set themselves up in defensive positions. The Royalist garrison sought to expel Fairfax from the churchyard, but with the arrival of Giffard they withdrew to the marketplace. Fairfax ordered Giffard to garrison the church and churchyard with his own men, using the surrounding wall for cover, and established an artillery battery by the church door. By now Sir William Fairfax and Foullis had pushed back the Royalist troops placed behind a barricade at Newton Bar and were emerging into the marketplace, or as we know it today, the Bull Ring. The Royalist forces were caught in a pincer movement, being fired on from Northgate and the churchyard. After offering the defenders a chance of surrender, which they

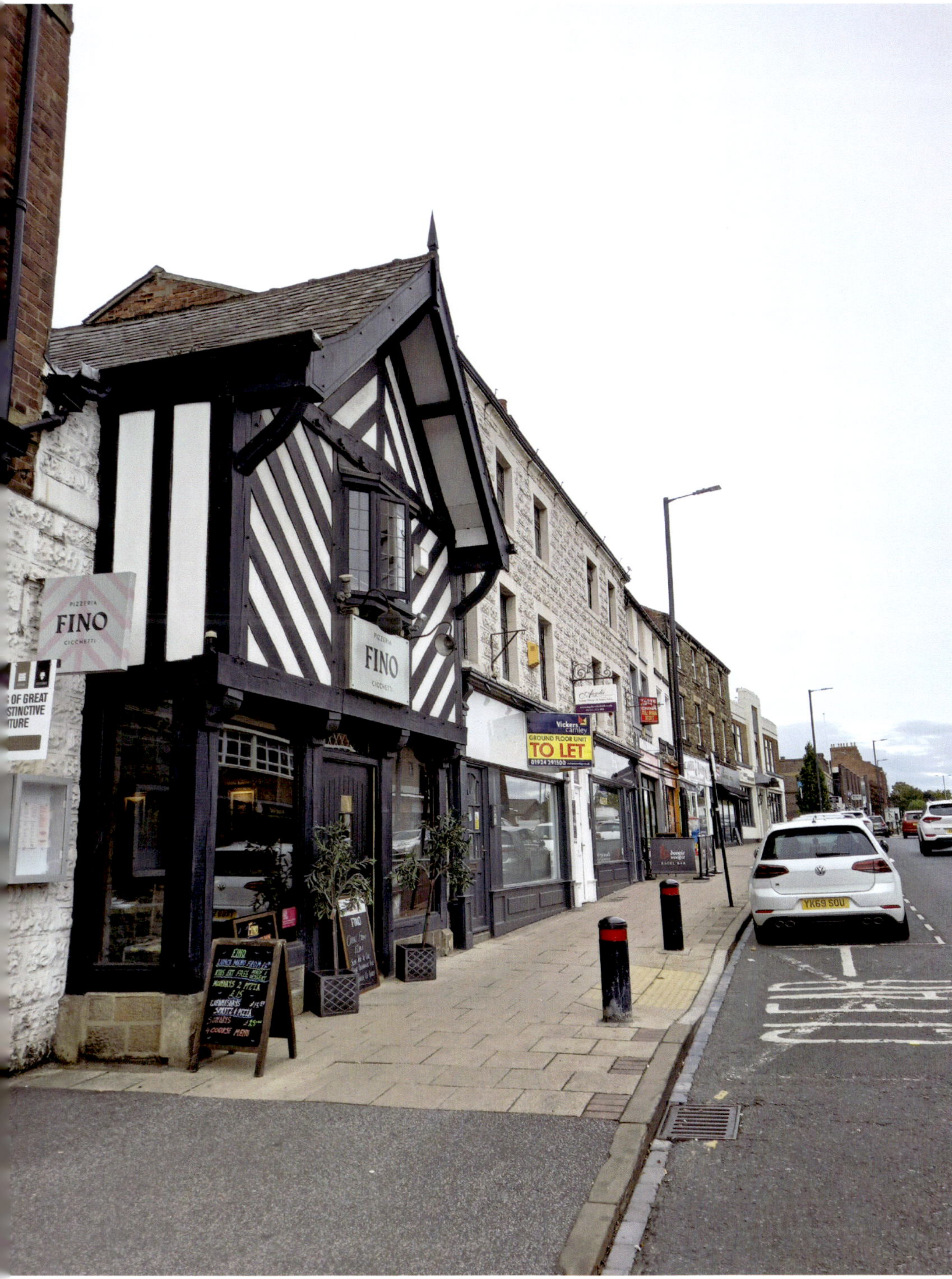

This timber-framed house on Northgate, built in the 1590s, witnessed Sir William Fairfax lead his cavalry down Northgate to attack the Yorkist troops assembled in what is now the Bull Ring.

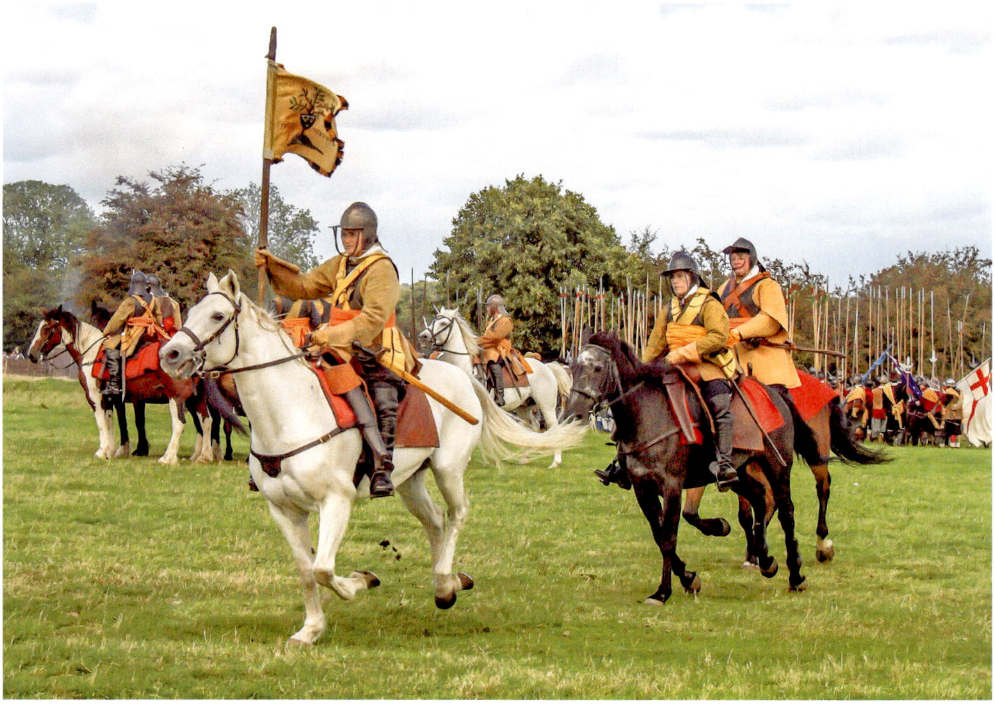

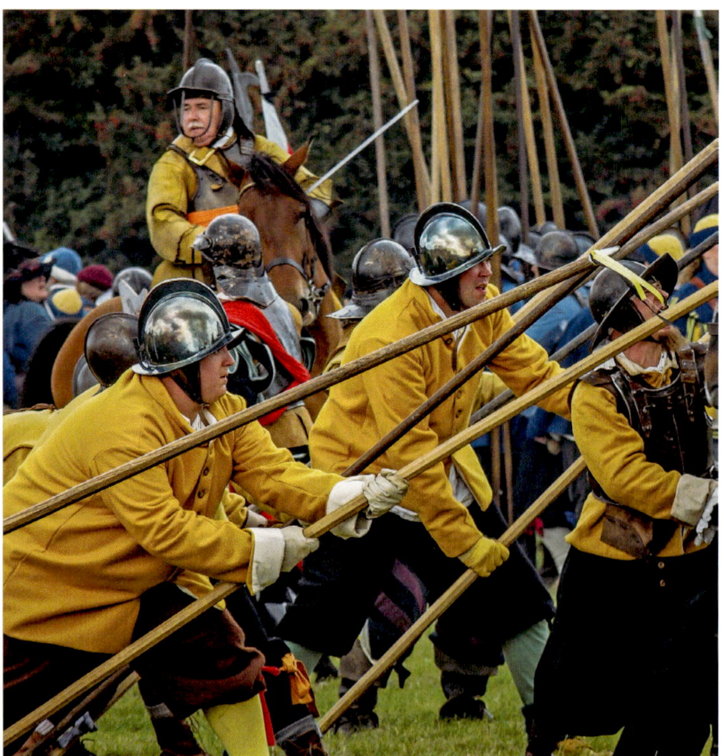

Above and left and opposite page: These re-enactors give a flavour of the dress and equipment of the two armies as they clashed in what today is the Bull Ring.

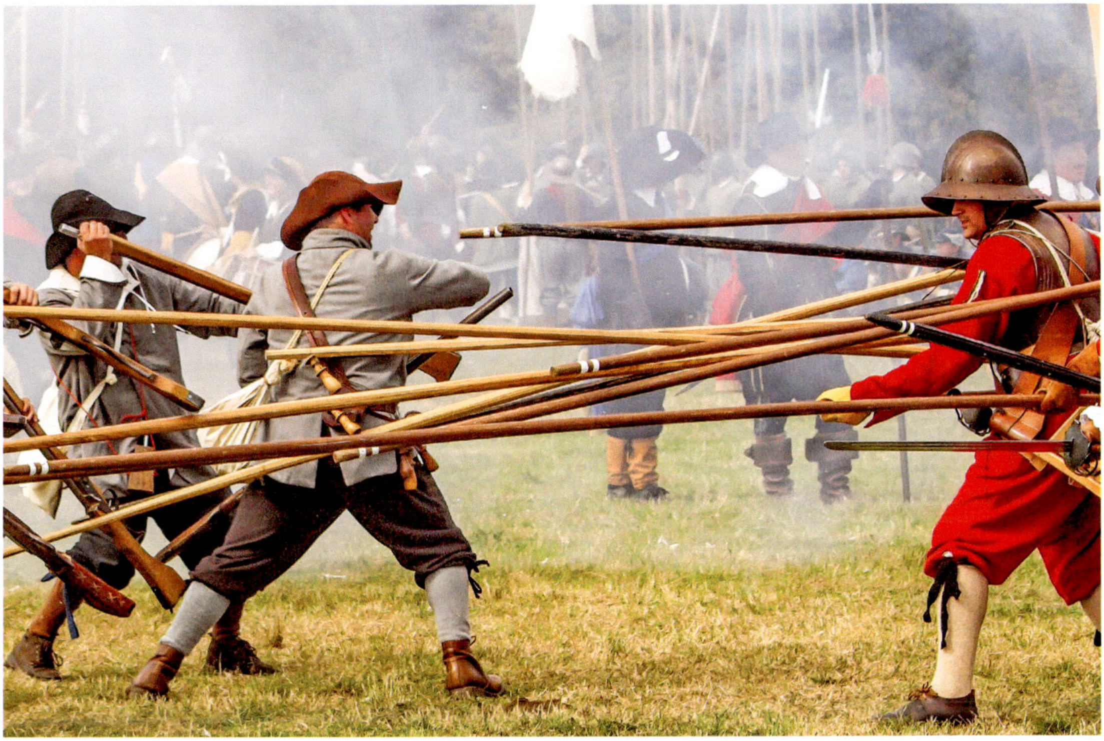

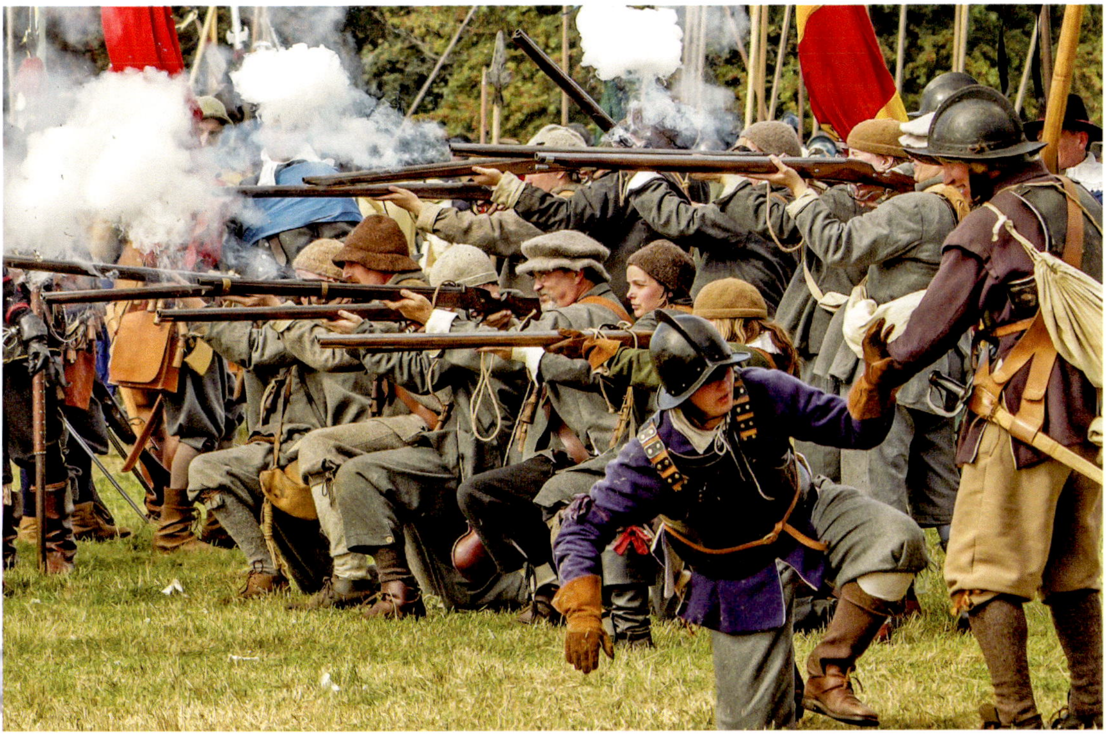

rejected, Sir Thomas Fairfax ordered his musketeers and artillery to open fire at almost point-blank range. Panicked, the Royalists fled along Westgate and were cut down by the Parliamentarian cavalry as they tried to flee. The remaining soldiers in the garrison gave up their resistance by 9 a.m.; the Parliamentarians held the town. Fairfax captured roughly 1,400 prisoners, including Goring, twenty-eight Royalist colours and a large amount of much-needed ammunition. After capturing Wakefield, Fairfax was wary of an attack from the larger Royalist army that Newcastle commanded, and he immediately retreated back to Leeds with his prisoners. Instead of the expected retaliation, Newcastle withdrew his own forces to York. In Parliament, Fairfax's news was read with jubilation on Sunday 27 May.

Taking of Wakefield

A Letter from my Lord Fairefax of the Three-and twentieth of May, and a Relation of the taking in of Wakefield, on Sunday last the One-and-twentieth of this Instant; wherein were taken Fifteen hundred common Soldiers, and Eight-and-thirty Commanders and Officers, and Colonel Goring General of the Horse; Four Pieces of Ordnance, the Ammunition: A List of the Officers, and a Relation inclosed, of the Manner of taking it, by a Party of Foot, and some Five hundred Horse, commanded in chief by Sir Tho. Fairefax, eldest Son to the Lord Fairefax, and Serjeant Major Gifford: And a Letter found in General Goring's Chamber, writ from his Father the Lord Goring:

Resolved, &c. That a publick Thanksgiving shall be given, in all the Churches and Chapels of London, Westminster, Borough of Southwark, and Suburbs, for the great and good Success it has pleased God to give the Forces under the Command of the Lord Fairfax, at the taking in of Wakefield.

Resolved, &c. That the Letter from the Lord Fairefax to Mr. Speaker; the Relation of taking in of Wakefield, under the Officers and Commanders Hands; the Names of the Officers taken Prisoners; the Letter from my Lord Goring to General Goring; be all forthwith printed, and read in Churches and Chapels: And Mr. Rous, and Mr. Millington, are appointed to prepare something to be printed with these Relations, by way of Introduction.

Resolved, &c. That it be especially recommended unto my Lord General to send, some effectual and speedy Succours to my Lord Fairefax, in such manner as shall seem best to his Excellency.

The Lords Concurrence to be desired herein, at a Conference: And Mr. Pym and Sir Hen. Vaine, are appointed Managers of that Conference.

Any advantage Fairfax had gained was nullified by his defeat at Adwalton Moor on 30 June.

Fighting did not return to Wakefield until spring 1645 when Sir Henry Poyntz at the head of Parliamentarian Army arrived to besiege Sandal Castle.

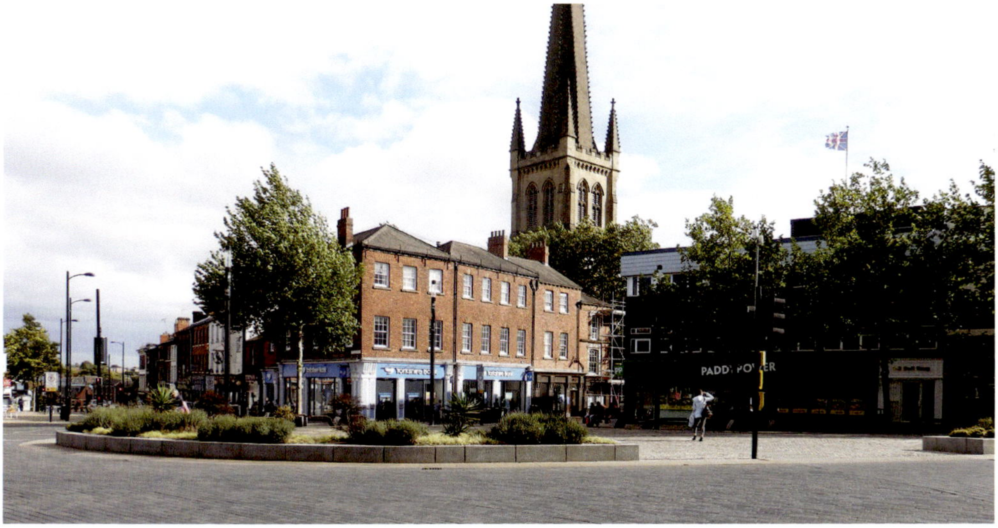

It is hard to imagine today that here, in the heart of Wakefield, a bloody battle was fought on 20 May 1643. Alas, the battle is almost totally unknown in Wakefield.

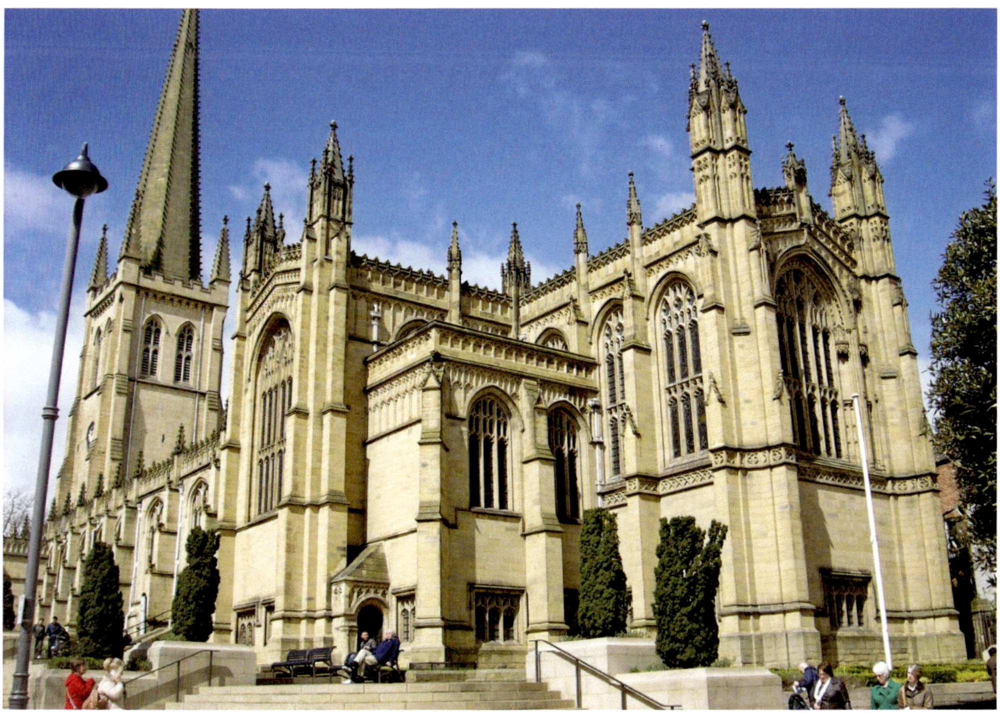

In the early hours of 20 May 1643, Sir Thomas Fairfax occupied our then parish church with his Parliamentarian forces. He established an artillery battery between the tower and north door, which fired into the then marketplace. The wall around the churchyard – now lost – became a firing step for the musketeers and dragoons to fire from against Yorkist forces, who tried to advance along Kirkgate and link with the force in the current Bull Ring.

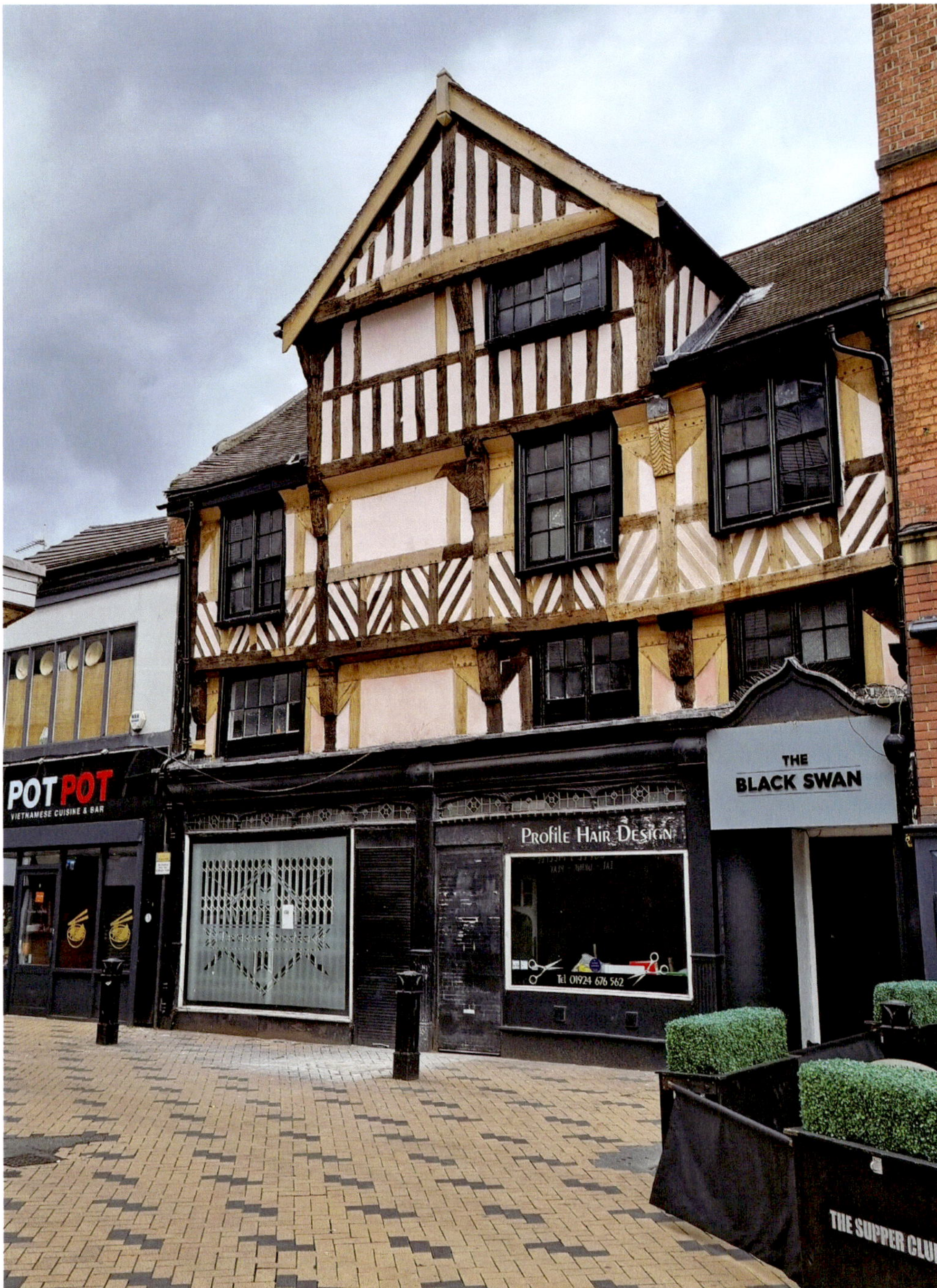

This timber-framed house on Silver Street, built between 1580 and 1620, witnessed the closing stages of the Battle of Wakefield. After offering the Yorkist force in the Bull Ring chance to surrender, which was refused, Sir Thomas Fairfax ordered his artillery to open fire at almost point-blank range. In the resulting panic, he charged 500 cavalry into the Bull Ring and routed the Royalists, who fled along Westgate. What stories of the battle could this old house tell us?

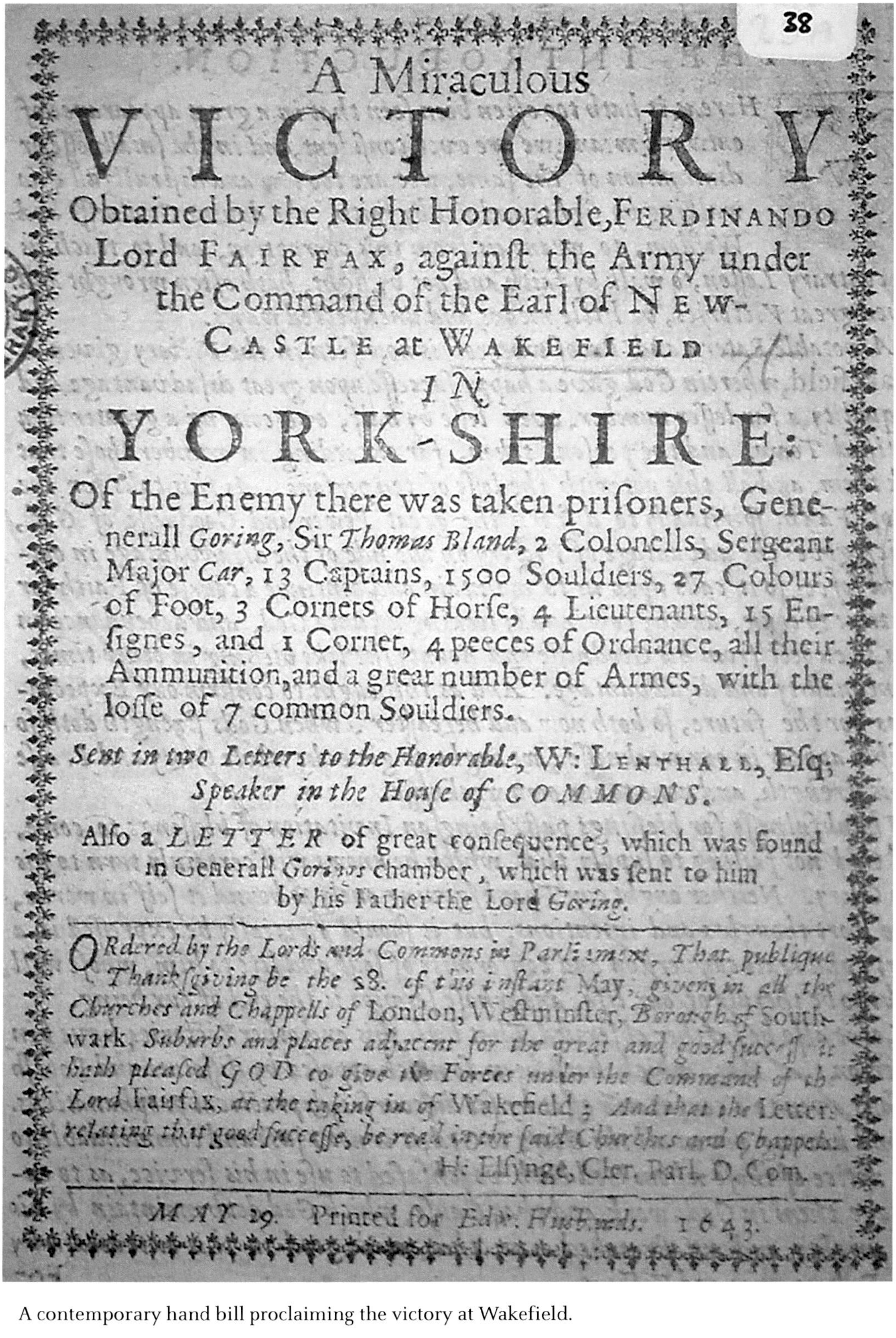

38

A Miraculous

VICTORY

Obtained by the Right Honorable, FERDINANDO Lord FAIRFAX, againſt the Army under the Command of the Earl of NEW-CASTLE at WAKEFIELD

IN

YORK-SHIRE:

Of the Enemy there was taken priſoners, Generall *Goring*, Sir *Thomas Bland*, 2 Colonells, Sergeant Major *Car*, 13 Captains, 1500 Souldiers, 27 Colours of Foot, 3 Corners of Horſe, 4 Lieutenants, 15 Enſignes, and 1 Cornet, 4 peeces of Ordnance, all their Ammunition, and a great number of Armes, with the loſſe of 7 common Souldiers.

Sent in two Letters to the Honorable, W: LENTHALL, Eſq; *Speaker in the Houſe of* COMMONS.

Alſo a *LETTER* of great conſequence, which was found in Generall *Gorings* chamber, which was ſent to him by his Father the Lord *Goring*.

ORdered by the Lords and Commons in Parliament, That publique Thankſgiving be the 28. of this inſtant May, given in all the Churches and Chappells of London, Weſtminſter, *Borough of* Southwark, *Suburbs and places adjacent for the great and good ſucceſſe it hath pleaſed GOD to give the Forces under the Command of the Lord* Fairfax, *at the taking in of* Wakefield; *And that the* Letters *relating that good ſucceſſe, be read in the ſaid Churches and Chappels.*

H: Elſynge, Cler. Parl. D. Com.

MAY 29. Printed for *Edw. Husbands.* 1643.

A contemporary hand bill proclaiming the victory at Wakefield.

The Siege of Sandal Castle

Since 1347, Sandal Castle had been in the hands of the Crown. The last monarch to invest in repairing the castle was Richard III during his short two-year reign. The incoming Tudor monarchy gave the castle little thought, especially after 1539 when the castle's administrative functions were centred at the Moot Hall on Kirkgate – the ancient manor house of the Earl Warenne, which survived (though heavily altered) until 1913. With no function, the castle fell into decay; by 1566 the great hall and principal buildings were roofless shells.

In 1638 the castle and its park were sold by the Crown to Francis Neville of Chevet – yes, the same family as the 1541 rebellion – for £1,110, described by this date as 'demolished or ruins'. The castle was surrounded on most sides by woodland. The inner moat, after being used as rubbish dump for 300 years, was little more than a shallow depression, with the outer moat likewise partially infilled, lined with oak trees and overgrown with shrubs such as hawthorn and bramble. The moat was far from defensive in nature. The few buildings in good condition included the kitchen (newly built in 1485), parts of the gatehouse and the undercrofts under the great hall and great chamber. In July 1644 these spaces were garrisoned by 200 Royalist infantry and perhaps eighty cavalry.

Re-analysis of the archaeological excavation of the castle by Anthony L. Dawson during 2002–03 notes that in the south-eastern quarter of the outer moat, an arrow-shaped bastion was constructed by cutting in to the southern moat bank to house four cannon overlooking the road to London. Outside the gatehouse, another gun emplacement was built of earth and earth-filled gabions, and a sixth position to the north-west of the motte. The south-eastern battery defended the castle's weakest side and where Sir John Saville, the first governor of the castle, felt the Parliamentarian threat would come from. By 1566, the great stone keep, last repaired in 1483–85, had no roof or floors and the walls were collapsing. It is very likely that the keep had collapsed, perhaps even by 1538, and had certainly collapsed by time of the siege in 1645. The defenders cut a trench through the demolition rubble connecting towers 2 and 4 (the well tower) with a temporary parapet built along the top of the trench for defence. Towers 2 and 3, or at least the basements, were occupied during the siege by the defenders based on the artefactual assemblage recovered. By the time of the siege the barbican tower had been deliberately dismantled and heavily robbed, and the stone carted away. Elimination of the keep and barbican would have greatly increased the space for the garrison and made the castle more defensive.

In the first week of May 1645, Royalist Captain John Benson and three of his men secretly left Pontefract Castle to strengthen the Sandal garrison, which had suffered eight men killed and several others wounded and captured when a foraging party had been ambushed by Parliamentarian forces. Sandal was encircled in January 1645, but the siege proper began during June by Parliamentarian forces. The initial Parliamentarian force of infantry with artillery – presented in the archaeological record of 9-pounder cannonballs – was supported by a force of 300 dragoons under Colonel Morgan. These were mounted infantry with matchlock muskets. However, with insufficient fodder for their horses, they could not continue the siege and withdrew to Pontefract.

On 22 July 1645, Parliament's Colonel General Poyntz called on the Royalist defenders to surrender, who refused. At the end of August, Colonel General Poyntz tightened the siege

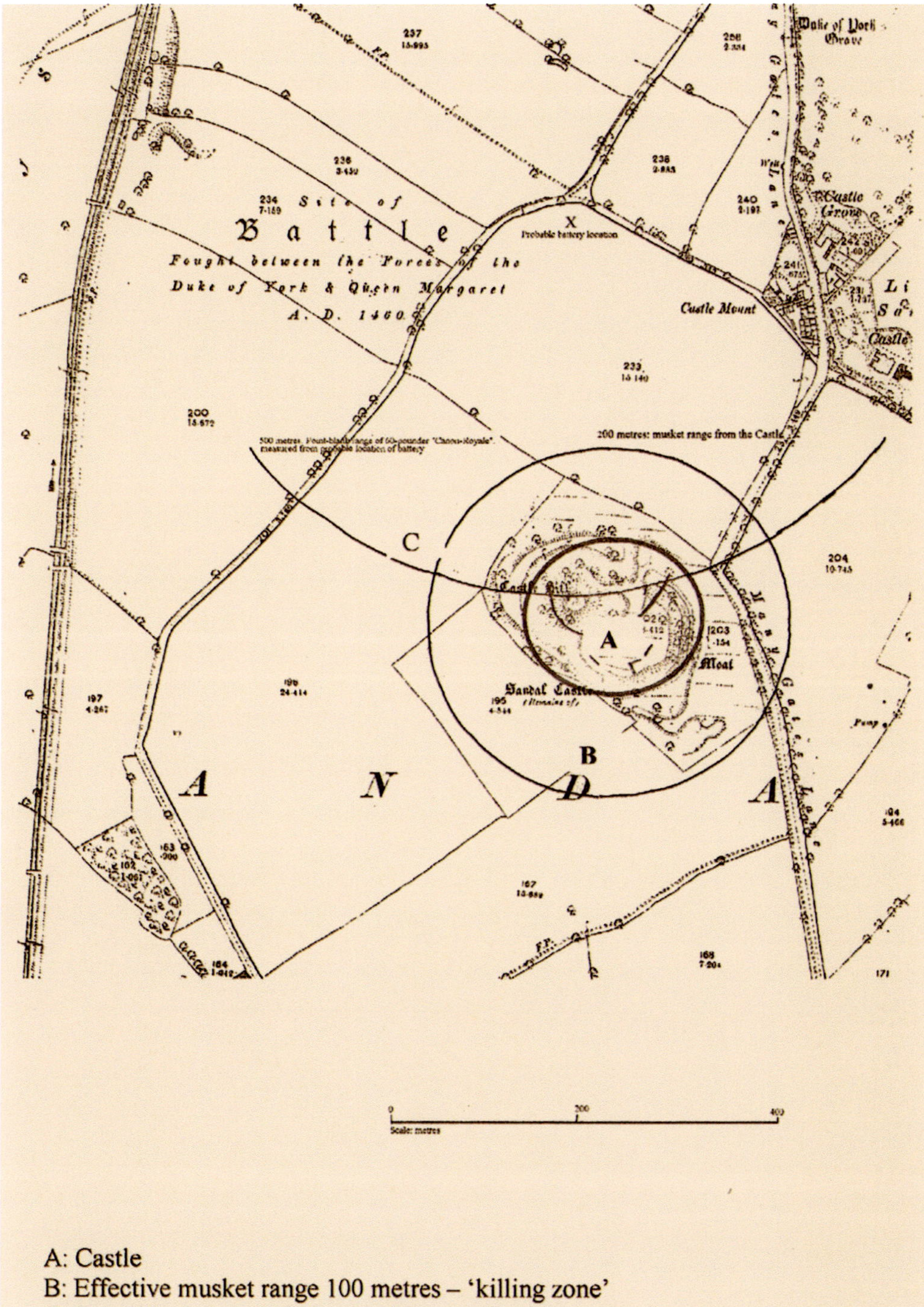

Map drawn by Anthony Dawson showing the location of the Civil War siege battery at Sandal. The pale around the park to the north of the castle provided the Parliamentarians with ready-made siege lines and covered way.

lines around Sandal Castle and obtained four great siege guns from Pontefract to bolster or replace the existing battery of smaller-calibre pieces. By now the Parliamentarian forces mustered over 5,000 men. The four guns, comprising a Cannon Royal 60 pounder, a 40 pounder, a 34 pounder and a 24 pounder, were manhandled into position with protection afforded them behind the medieval park and hedge. More than forty cannonballs and other artillery projectiles were recovered in excavations. The two main targets for the battery appear to have been the motte and gatehouse. The curtain wall between these structures was also targeted. Shot found in the barbican 'ditch' and in the courtyard behind these two structures had likely been fired into the castle but missed their mark.

Anthony Dawson reports that archaeology and textual reference report a major fire in the castle at this stage. It is likely to have been the constables' lodgings, which were timber framed and have set fire by mortar shells, some fragments of which were recovered archaeologically. The burnt shell of this building, and others that had been burned out, were demolished and some of the materials were then used to construct a rubble-filled bank butting to the inner face of the curtain wall between the gatehouse and great chamber where the medieval wall had collapsed. The battery was in action for twenty-five days or more.

After several breaches had been made in the walls of the castle, on 30 September 1645 Parliament's Colonel Robert Overton made preparations to storm Sandal Castle, but after a parley the defenders agreed to leave on favourable terms. On 1 October (some sources say the 3rd) 1645, Colonel Bonivant surrendered the Royalist garrison at Sandal at 10 a.m. By now, the garrison consisted of ten officers and ninety men – more than half of the garrison had been killed. The horses had been eaten. The majority of the men had been killed in April and May, showing that hand-to-hand combat took place, as well as formal siege lines. Had the castle been attacked with a forlorn hope in a desperate attempt to take the castle by storm before the siege guns came up?

Sixty-three Royalists were killed and 183 captured in April, compared to forty-two Parliamentarians killed, fifty wounded and fifty made prisoner. Both sides, in total, lost 128 men killed, with fifty-eight wounded and 268 taken prisoner. The garrison included women and children – a baby's dummy recovered archaeologically is unequivocal proof of this. We do not know if mother and child survived the siege. The remaining garrison surrendered 100 muskets, fifty pikes, twenty halberds, 150 swords and two barrels of gunpowder. No artillery was mentioned in the inventory. The Royalist defenders marched to Welbeck House in north Nottinghamshire. What remained of the castle was demolished during 1646/47. In all probability, there was likely little left to pull down.

With the coming of peace, Wakefield would become home to a distinguished Parliamentarian officer, Captain Joseph Poole (we mentioned him earlier). Poole, a friend of Cromwell and radical Sir John Lambert, had commanded the artillery during the last siege of Pontefract in 1649. He may have been at Sandal in 1645. Poole was a religious Dissenter and a key person in the founding of the Dissenters' meeting house on Westgate Common in 1697. His daughter Baptista married the minister here, Revd Joseph Sagar. And his other daughter, Hannah, married Robert Milnes, a wealthy cloth merchant. Poole died in 1703 and is buried in the Quaker cemetery on Doncaster Road. Hannah and Robert were buried in the cemetery around the Westgate Common Chapel. The Milnes family would come to dominate Wakefield until the early twentieth century.

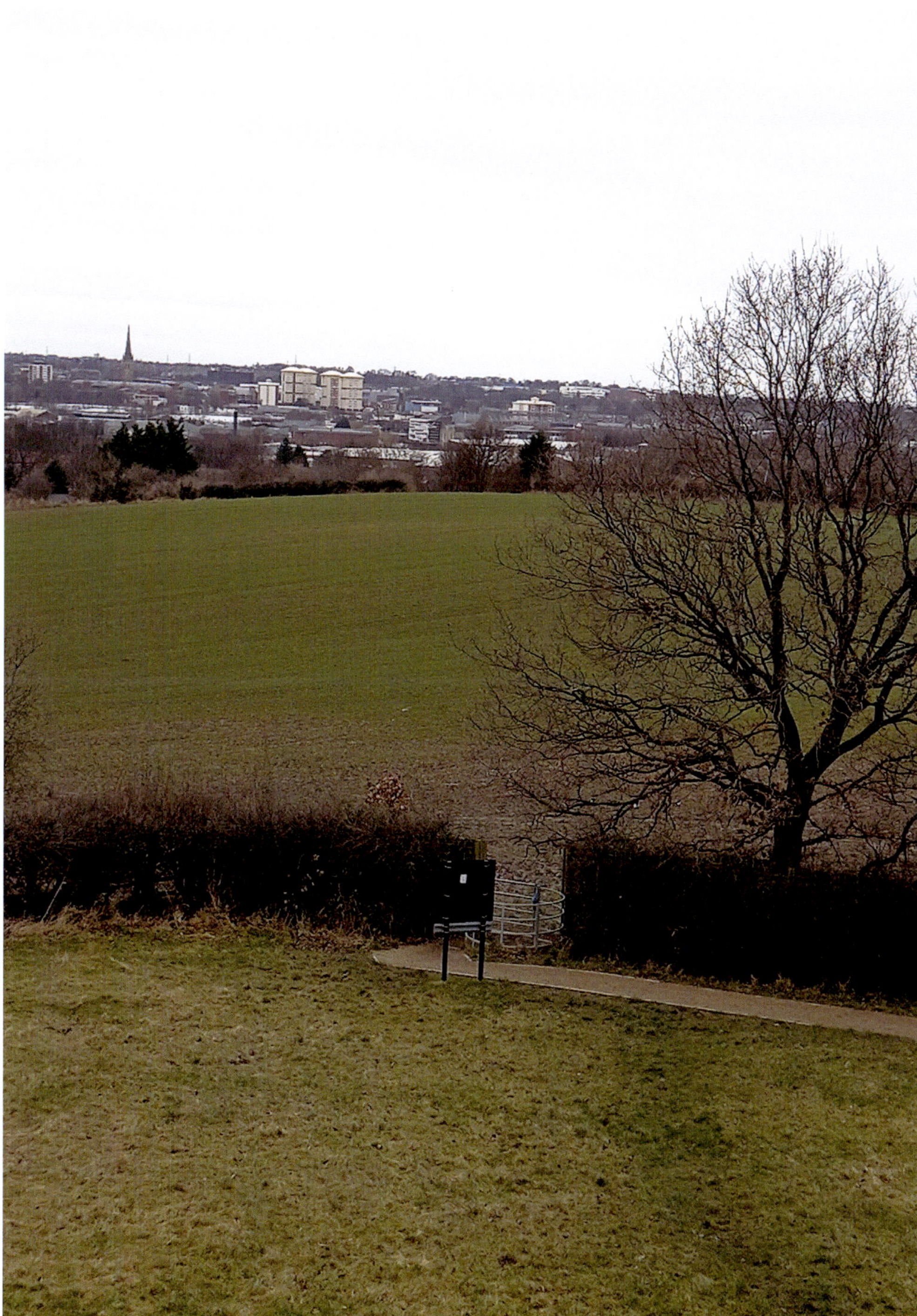

Looking north to Wakefield across the Royalist lines – marked by a hedge – to the Parliamentarian siege battery marked the by copse in the middle of the image. The hedge and tree line mark the substantial bank and ditch around the medieval deer park which surrounded the castle.

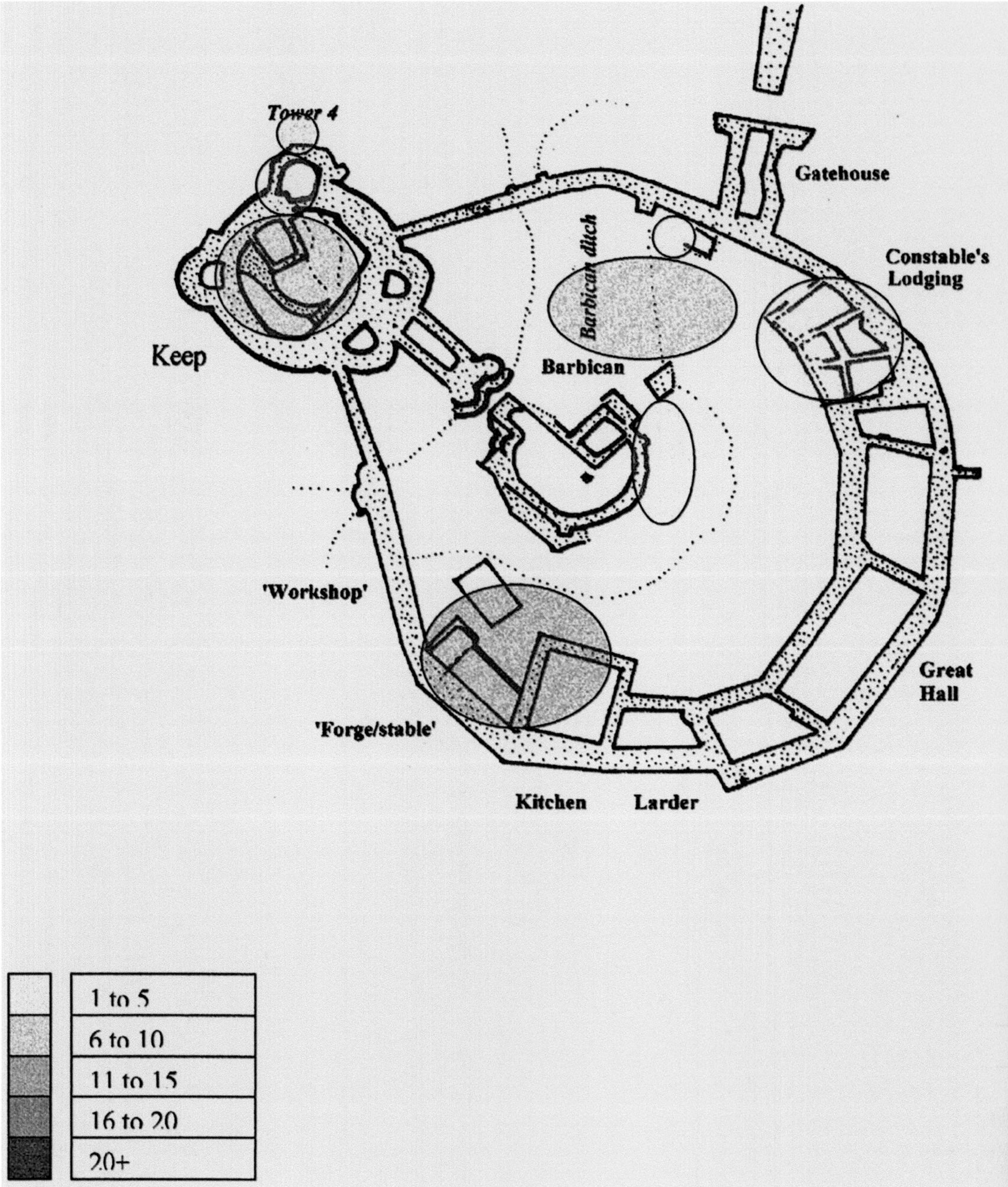

Map by Anthony Dawson showing the distribution of lead shot recovered from Sandal Castle during the archaeological excavations. The distribution could suggest shot production in the former kitchen block.

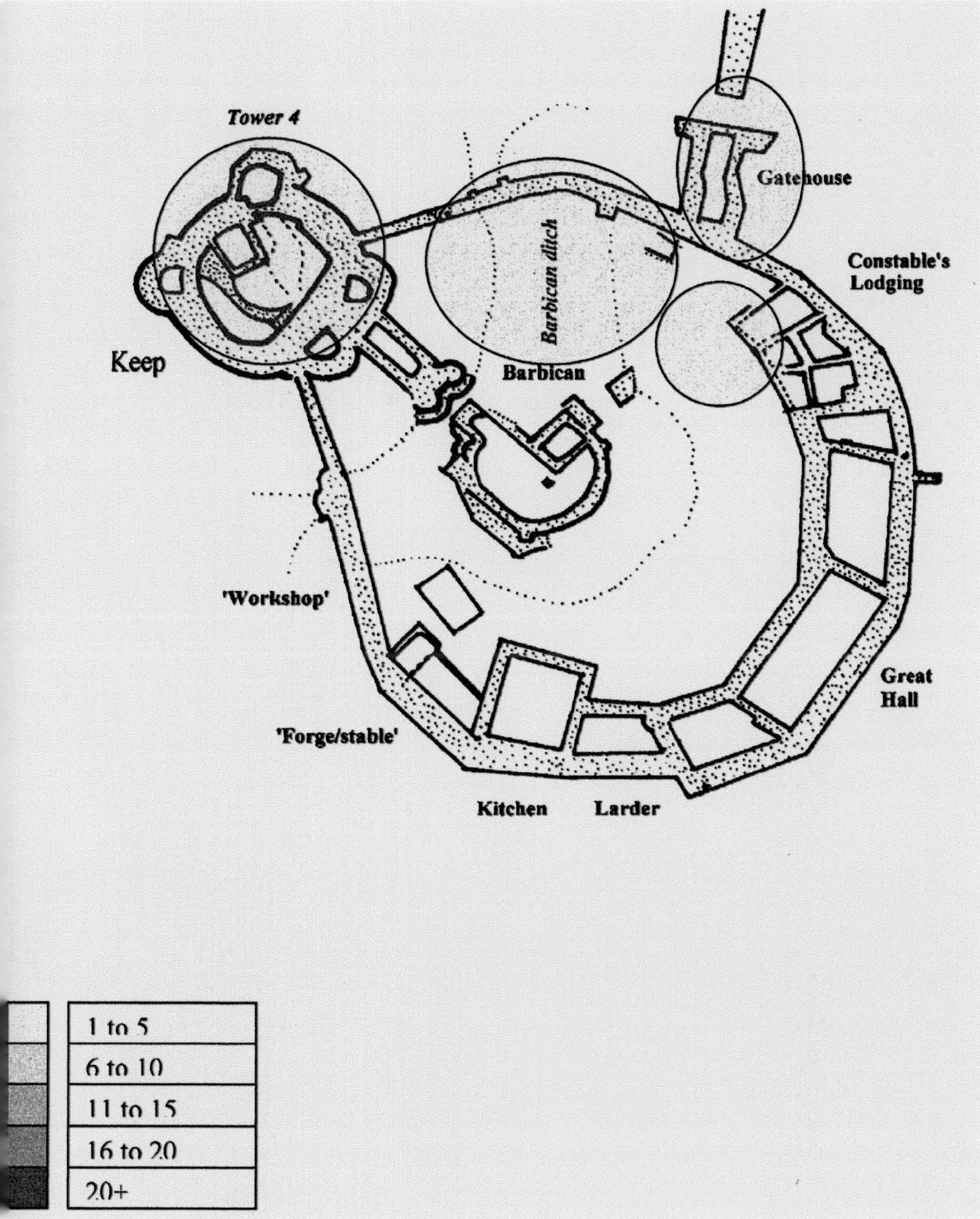

Map by Anthony Dawson showing the distribution of iron recovered from Sandal Castle during the archaeological excavations.

5. Wars Against France

When the monarchy was restored in 1660, a key aspect was its reliance on a standing army and the use of repressive legislation to maintain its power. The abortive rebellion of 1659 had demonstrated the need for a standing army. The suppression of the Monmouth Rebellion and civil war in Ireland against James II following the last successful invasion of the country by the Dutch, led by William of Orange, as two examples. The tensions leading to these internal conflicts were by and large religious. Tensions boiled over in 1662, when a resurgent Church of England excommunicated over 2,000 priests and perhaps 20,000 lay members of the Church on the grounds of Church governance and theology. The State, through legislation, sought to eliminate dissent from Church and State. As historian Susan Loughlan writes, the great innovation of Henry VIII was to assimilate loyalty to the Crown with loyalty to the Church of England. Loyalism and nationhood became bound to religious identity. Dissention from the Church of England meant, in very simple terms, disloyalty and therefore treason. The Crown, therefore, through the Test and Corporation Acts and later the Blasphemy Act, sought to legislate dissent into non-existence.

Whatever the intention of the Crown, and also the House of Bishops in a restored House of Lords, dissent did not acquiesce. While the State was divided between subjects of two distinct legal statuses, tension remained. Those made 'second class' by their faith understandably sought to overturn the legislation – and therefore the Crown – in seeking equality. Religious dissent would dominate the socio-economic political development of Wakefield, along with the major urban centres of Leeds, Halifax and Sheffield until the years before the Second World War. Tensions between Dissenters and the Establishment, however, boiled over.

Religion as much as politics resulted in Britain and France being at war for over 100 years, with interludes of peace, until 1815.

For both internal defence and to provide an army reserve, in 1680, during the reign of Charles II, a Militia Act was passed. Largely based on an Act of Henry VIII from 1539, each parish had to provide a quota of men and equipment for the militia, which was intended to provide a local defence force. The system had shortcomings but continued on, albeit with some changes and periods of inactivity, until the Milita Act of 1757. In Wakefield, the Town Constable's book, kept in the John Goodchild collection, reports the expenses for the upkeep of the militia in the town. In 1681, Benjamin Johnson and William Lawson had £20 to buy muskets; Daniel Hoyle gave £12; Thomas Pease gave £4, Richard Shaw, £6; Zachary Moor, £6 13*s* 4*d*; Rebecca Oley, £3; and George Witherspin, Richard Norfolk and William Howard, £12. Corslets (a breast and back plate with hinged metal plates covering the thighs) were given by Richard Ellis, John Maud, Samuel Liversage, Thomas Harris, Mabell Naylor, Widow Thompson, Miss Green Wood, John Scott and others. They were worn by pikemen. We note John Milnes gave £2 10*s* for a corslet. In total, the townsfolk

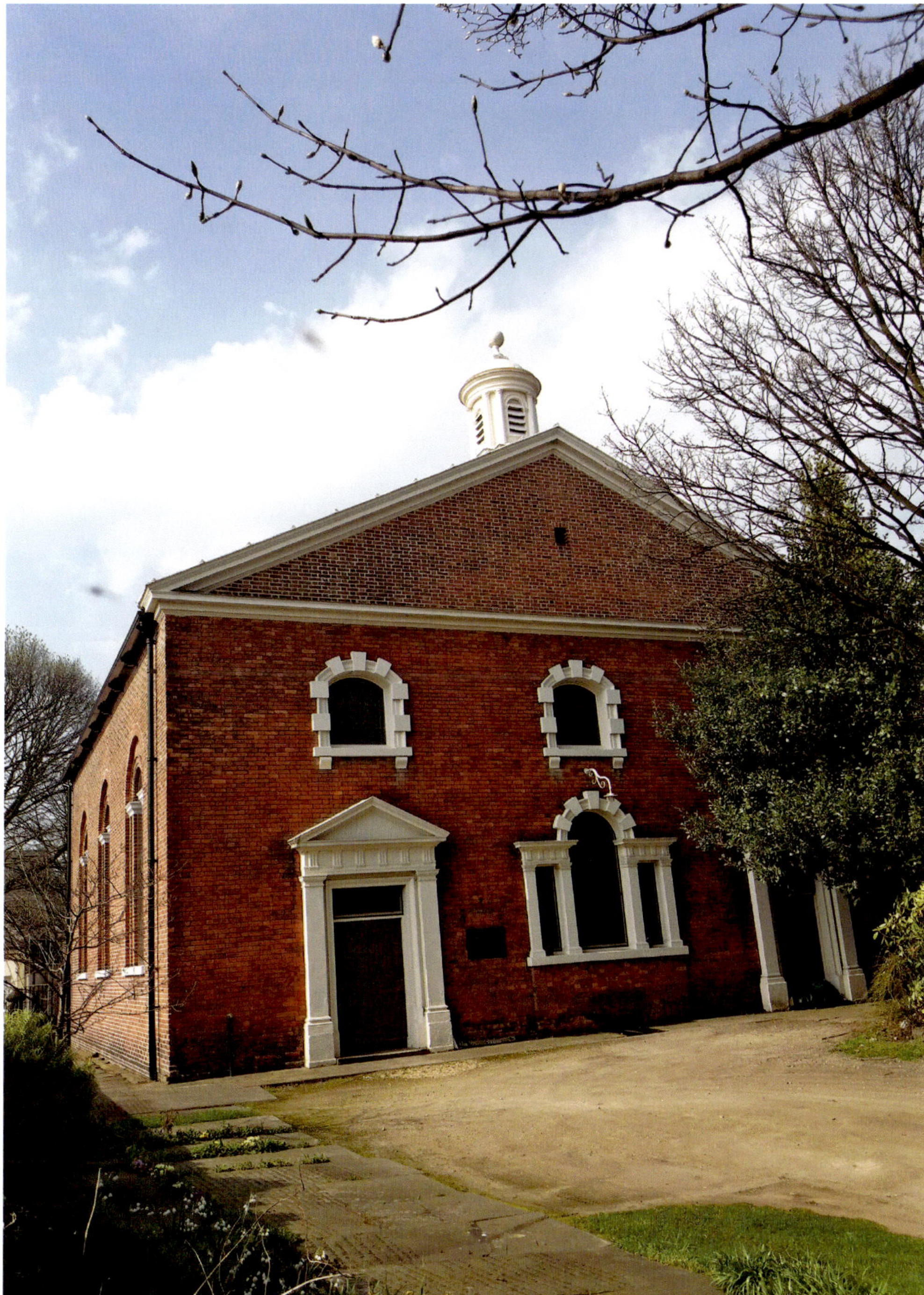

Westgate Chapel, completed in 1752, replaced an earlier chapel of 1697. This in turn replaced a meeting house on George Street, which opened in May 1672. For much of the eighteenth and nineteenth centuries, the Milnes family and relatives dominated the congregation and mercantile development of Wakefield.

gave twenty-nine donations for corslets and forty for muskets. In all, almost £600 was raised to arm the militia. Men were chosen for the militia by a ballot and had to serve for a fixed term. The ballot became hated, but the militia did prove its worth.

Politics and religion were behind the events of 1715. The 1688 Glorious Revolution deposed James II and VII, who was replaced by his Protestant daughter, Mary II, and her Dutch husband, William III, ruling as joint monarchs. Shortly before William's death in March 1702, the Act of Settlement 1701 definitively excluded Catholics from the throne. This included James's son, James Francis Edward Stuart. Since his Protestant half-sister Anne (r. 1702–14) had no surviving children, the Act named her successor as the distantly related – but, importantly, Protestant – Sophia of Hanover. However, she died in July 1714, so when Anne herself died in August it was Sophia's eldest son, George, who became monarch. Many were opposed to the settlement and gathered around James Stuart.

The 1710–14 Tory government had actively prosecuted their Whig opponents, Catholics and Dissenters, and tipped the nation towards civil war. The Scots and their English supporters defeated Crown forces at the Battle of Preston on 12–14 November. The government landed 3,000 Dutch troops in London and 3,000 in Hull to defend the Protestant ascendancy. To guard hearth and home, the Town Constable's register records £100 expended for repairing muskets, as well as for paying the Waites – an early police force – for enforcing a curfew. The rebellion was over by January 1716.

Wakefield and Bonnie Prince Charlie

A generation later religious and political factors once more led to another attempt to oust the Hanoverian monarchy in favour of the Stuarts. Since March 1744, France had been at war with Great Britain. The French sought to harness remaining anger against the Hanoverians and the Act of Union of Scotland and England by supporting Bonnie Prince Charlie, financially and militarily, to invade. Since 1715, the Whig party and Dissenters had been drawn together in an alliance opposed to Tory Anglicanism. Perhaps unsurprisingly, many blamed Dissenters for the events of 1715 and 1745: divisions between Church and Dissent, and the alliance between religious dissent and political dissention, it was argued, had left the country vulnerable to an invasion by Catholics.

With Charles Edward Stuart's victory over the Hanoverian army at Prestonpans on 20 September 1745, panic gripped the north of England as the victorious army headed south. In Wakefield, Richard Milnes led a county-wide subscription for finances and assisted forming a body of volunteers to defend hearth and home. We note John Milnes gave £30, John Milnes & Co. gave £30 and Richard gave £50; in total, £355 16*s* was raised. Similar actions would be taken by the family half a century later for the same reasons. As a merchant and man of wealth, Richard had a lot to lose if the Hanoverian dynasty was displaced. History tells us that the Highlanders reached Derby and then turned back. Drawing on his contacts in Edinburgh and Newcastle, during the rebellion Milnes submitted reports to the 1st Marquess of Rockingham and made a close friend of the 2nd Marquess, Charles Lord Higham, as he then was. In gathering information, Milnes was not afraid to employ 'scouts' (spies?) to gather information that he could send onto the county elite:

> 1745, Dec. 2. Wakefield. Three scouts, who returned from Manchester last night, report that the rebels began their march thence to Stockport and Knutsford yesterday morning at 4 o'clock. One of my men stayed at Manchester till 10.30 and saw all the foot gone. Some horse, being the rear-guard, were in town when he came away and would not march as he apprehended, till this day. They gave out that their march would be directly for London, but it was thought they would make for Chester or Wales.

Milnes, as a self-appointed informant for the Crown, became a key conduit for information. Rather than heading to London, on reaching Derby the Highlanders headed north. Richard wrote to Lord Irwin, Lord Lieutenant at Temple Newsome, on 9 December 1745:

> The main body of the rebels was at Ashburn last Friday night where an acquaintance of mine and about 39 persons were tried by court martial for spies. Thirty of them were acquitted and discharged and ten kept in confinement for farther trial. My friend got here yesterday at noon. He had been carried prisoner from Manchester to Derby and back to Ashburn, where he left them on their march for Leek and Macclesfield. I have just now seen another person who saw about 500 of them at Stockport on Saturday night.
>
> The whole body of the rebels was expected in Manchester last night, but were not there at 9 o'clock. The people in that town are all arming themselves, as is the whole country all along the roads where the highlanders are expected to pass in order to attack them on their retreat, being greatly enraged at the ill-usage they met as they advanced. Marshal Wade's army is to encamp here tomorrow night. Colonel Du Rour is come to mark out the camp. I shall send the breeches for the east riding companies by the next carrier.

On 10 December, Marshall Wade arrived in Wakefield from Newcastle with 8,000 British and 6,000 Dutch troops. Wade had marched south on hearing news the Highlanders were seeking to evade the army led by the Duke of Cumberland. Wade left on 11 December, heading to Preston. It was to Sir Rowland Winn, 4th Baronet, that he wrote from Berwick with an account of Culloden on 20 April 1746:

> The Duke has got a compleat victory over the Rebels at Cowden Hill near Inverness, most if the High Landers are cut to pieces & the remainder are fled, all their cannon are taken. Lord George Murray, Lord Kilmarnock & Sir John Wedderburn with the French Embassador are taken prisoner.

Four days later, Milnes wrote again: 'I hope notwithstanding there not be so many killed &n taken prisoner as the news first told, that yet the victory is so compleat that they will never more be able to shew their heads but must disperse.' Milnes died in 1755. He was buried beneath Westgate Chapel, which he had largely financed. His sons would go on to be important members of Wakefield's social, cultural, religious and economic life.

Volunteer Soldiers

In 1757, the Militia Act brought substantial changes, creating a far more professional force. County regiments, Monmouthshire included, were smaller and better trained than the militia had been in the past. Rather than all men being expected to serve, a number were selected by ballot to serve for three years, although it was possible for those who were selected to avoid service by paying for a substitute. Officers were appointed by the lord lieutenant of the county and were from the higher social classes. Most importantly, the regiments were 'embodied' (assembled) from time to time for training.

The militia could only be deployed at home, but they provided an important contribution to the maintenance of civil order and home defence. Under the Act, the West Yorkshire Militia were formed in Leeds. The three original battalions of 1757 were reorganised two years later into three regiments. The 1st was commanded by Colonel Lord Downe (Henry Pleydell Dawnay, Viscount Downe), raised in the Wapentakes of Osgoldcross, Strafforth and Tickhill, Staincross, Barkston Ash and part of Skyrack; it was actually the last to be organised, its officers being commissioned on 29 June 1759. Colonel Sir George Savile's 2nd, raised in the Wapentakes of Agbrigg and Morley, was the second organised, with commissions dated 13 February 1760. Colonel William Thornton's 3rd was raised in the Wapentakes of Claro, Staincliffe and Ewecross, the earliest to complete, its commissions dated 27 January 1760. All three regiments were disembodied in December 1762. In 1763 the three undersized regiments were reorganised into two stronger, ten company, regiments: the 1st, or Southern, Regiment under Colonel Sir George Savile, and the 2nd, or Northern, under Colonel William Thornton, effectively making the previous 2nd the new 1st, and the previous 3rd the new 2nd. The 1st, like the 2nd, was re-embodied in March 1778 during the American War, and disembodied in 1783. With the commencement of war with France in 1793, the 1st Regiment was re-embodied in early 1793 under Colonel Charles Howard, Duke of Norfolk, who was dismissed by the king in 1798 as lord lieutenant for favouring democratic ideas. The 2nd and 3rd regiments were raised simultaneously. In 1797 three regiments of Supplementary Militia were raised, initially numbered as the 1st to 3rd Supplementary, but promptly re-numbered as the 3rd to 5th 'regular' Militia; when the 3rd and 4th were disembodied in 1799, the 5th became the new 3rd.

From 1794 the militia were joined by more part-time soldiers: the country yeomanry and the Royal Wakefield Volunteers. The unit had been formed when Benjamin Kennet, Wakefield Town Constable for 1794, called a meeting in the Moot Hall on 19 May 1794 of the 'Clergy, Gentlemen and Merchants, Traders and respectable Merchants of the Town' for the purpose of forming a volunteer corps for the 'internal defence of this town and neighbourhood, against insurrection of any commotion'.

David Parkhill was named drill instructor of the new corps. Parkhill was a veteran of the American Revolutionary Wars and had been gazetted captain on 17 January 1761 in the 41st Regiment of Foot. He had served as a lieutenant in 1757 at Minden. He served

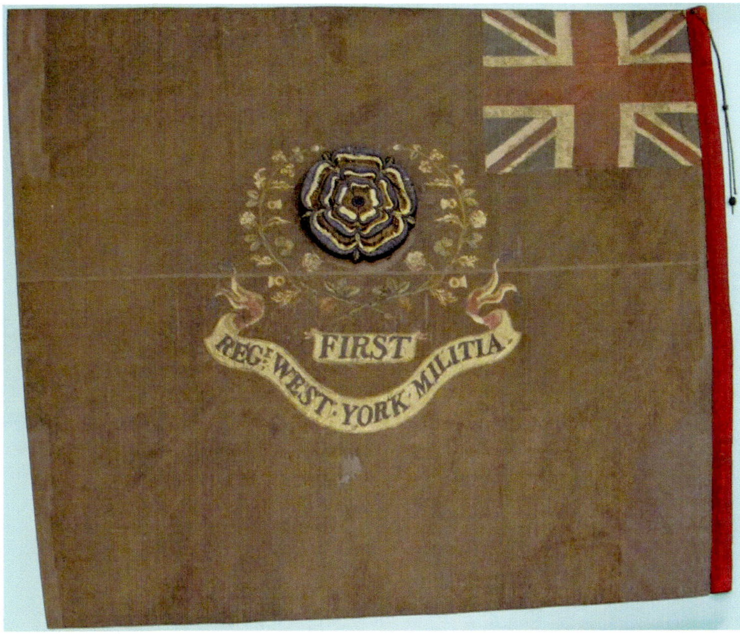

Colours of the 1st Battalion West Riding Militia dating from the 1760s.

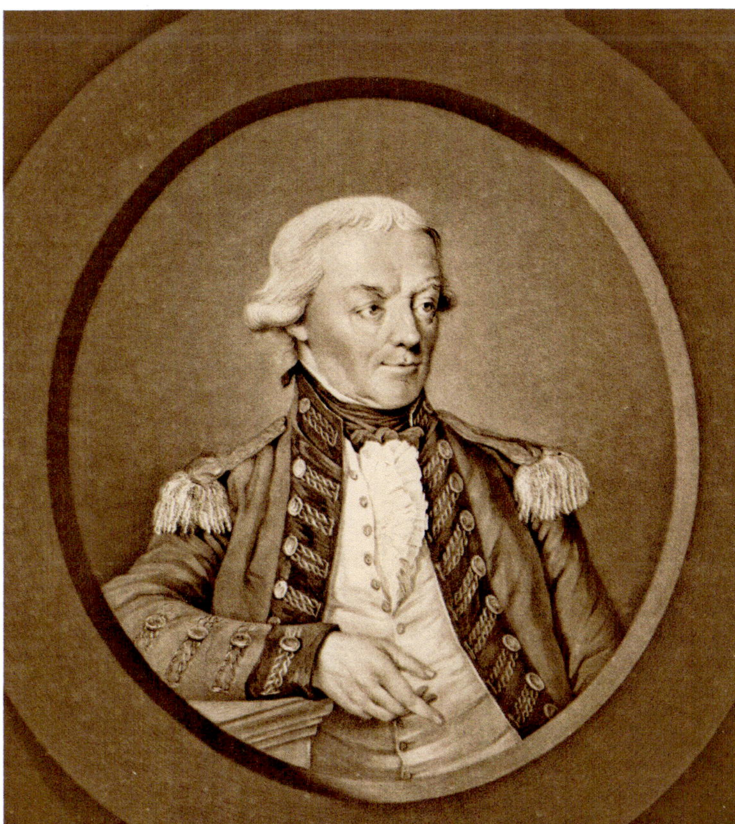

Colonel Robert Prescott, a veteran officer of the Seven Years' War and American Revolutionary Wars.

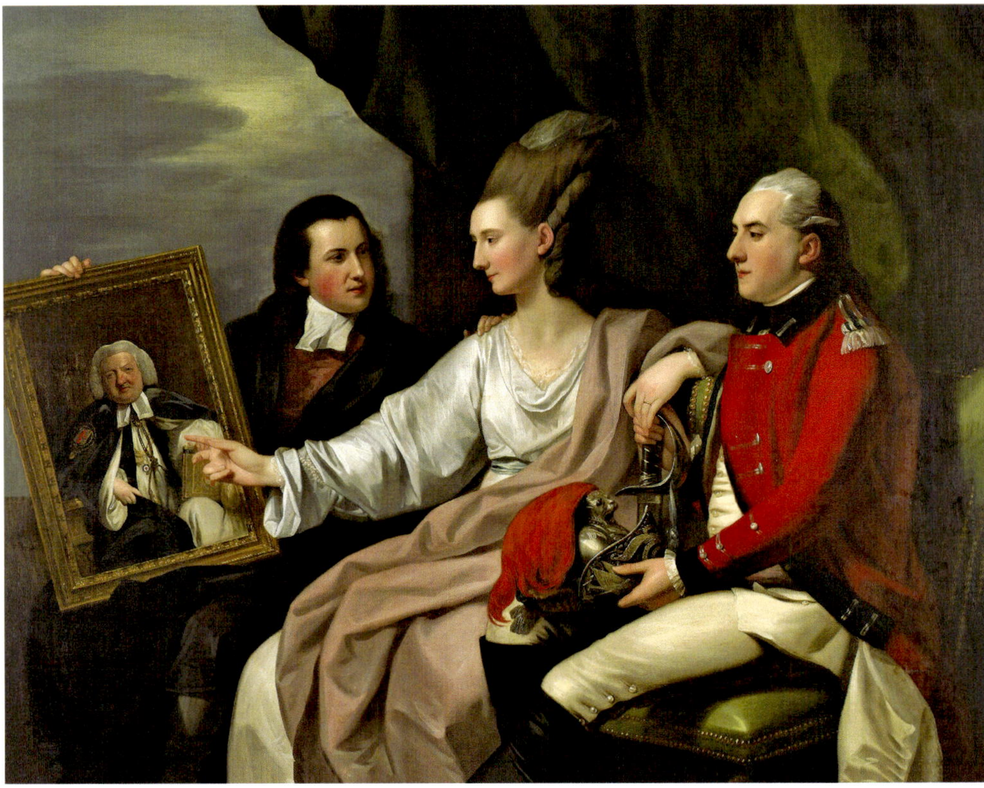

Mary Bridgette Milnes, only child of Pemberton Milnes, shown seated alongside her husband, Peter Auriol Hey Drummond, Colonel of West Riding Militia. Her father-in-law, Archbishop Drummond of York, is in the small portrait. The pair met at the archbishop's home of Brodsworth Hall near Doncaster. Her father, Pemberton, built both Pemberton House in Wakefield and Bawtry Hall, close to Doncaster. Mary Bridgette lies in the catacombs with her father beneath Westgate Chapel.

in the 12th Regiment of Foot during the America War and was invalided out on full pay. His son was Lieutenant Colonel Parkhill of the 35th Regiment of Foot. He was a fully paid-up member of Westgate Chapel, which was founded in 1661 as Presbyterian but by the mid-eighteenth century became increasingly Unitarian in theology. In 1794, he is recorded as renting pews 31 and 32, paying £5 3*s* per year subscription. From January 1795 his attendance became sporadic, paying £1 5*s* 6*d*. He lies buried in Wakefield Parish Church, a good Anglican.

These part-time soldiers were called into action on 6 August 1795 at the height of a famine. Marching from Wakefield to Knottingley, they faced down an angry mob. Chief among the protagonists was a collier by the name of Michael Sidebottom. Having yelled at the troops that they would not escape alive, at one point he grabbed the reins of a Pontefract cavalryman's horse, tried to drag it towards the river and kept hold until the bucking animal unseated its rider. Also in the thick of the action were two women: Ann Sharp, the wife of a Castleford boatman, and Margaret Wilson from Methley. Sheircliffe Smith, a Pontefract saddler, was charged with assault of George Pearson, a trooper in

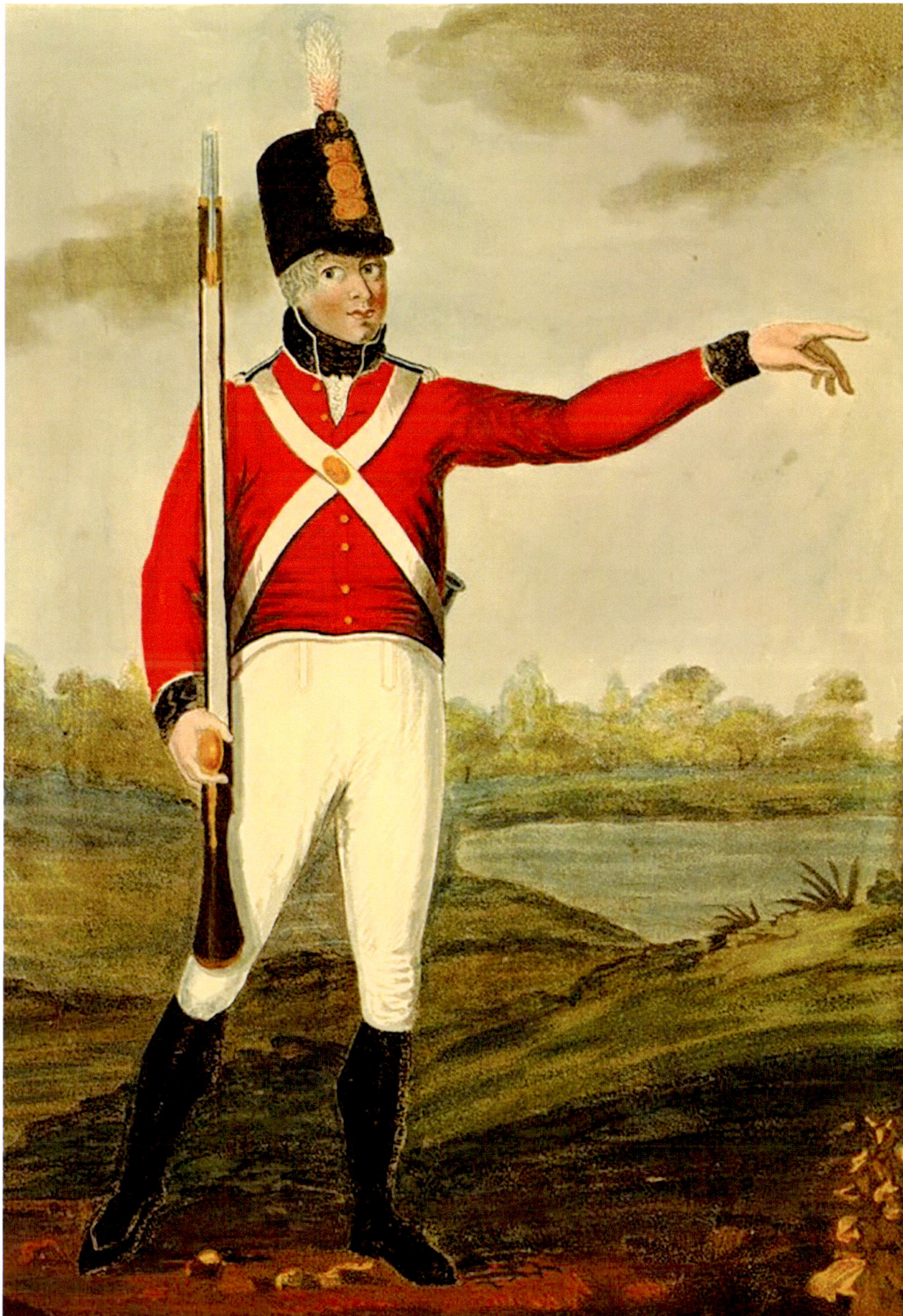

Raised in 1794 until stood down in 1802 and hastily reformed in 1803, the Royal Wakefield Volunteers were dressed in similar manner between 1802 and 1814.

the Pontefract troop of yeomanry cavalry. In all, a dozen people were arrested. Of the villagers arrested, Michael Sidebottom, Ann Sharp and Margaret Wilson were remanded in York Castle (the two women were held on the word of David Dunderdale, who must have observed the events happening alongside his premises, and Sidebottom on the oath of a Captain Jeremiah Naylor), while another three were sent to Wakefield Prison. Sidebottom was charged with riotous behaviour and threatening the lives of the soldiers, while Sharp and Wilson were accused of aiding and assisting the detention of the vessel; the latter two were released on bail, but Michael Sidebottom remained in custody at York, with all three set to stand trial at York Assizes the following spring.

The volunteers were called out again in 1800 to supress a food riot. They were supported by the Wakefield Volunteer Cavalry, formed from the wealthiest men of the town to defend their property from the dispossessed poor. The Royal Wakefield Volunteers and the militia were stood down in 1802, but with war against Napoleon being declared in 1803, they were called up once more. The Royal Wakefield Volunteers were in action again in 1812 when they opened fire on Luddites returning from the raid on Cartwright's Mill in Horbury. They were stood down at the end of 1816.

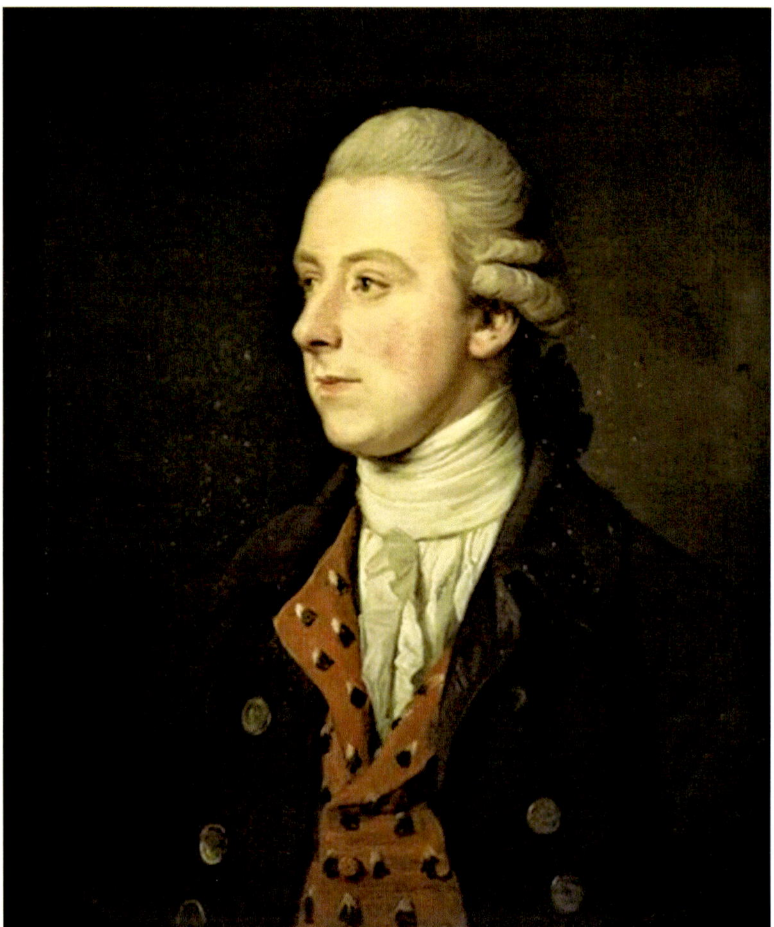

James Milnes, for whom Thorne House was built, raised his own troop of volunteer cavalry in 1798 to defend 'hearth and home' from the threat of invasion by the French. His troop of cavalry galloped into action in spring 1800 to put down a bread riot in Wakefield marketplace. He lies in the catacombs beneath Westgate Chapel.

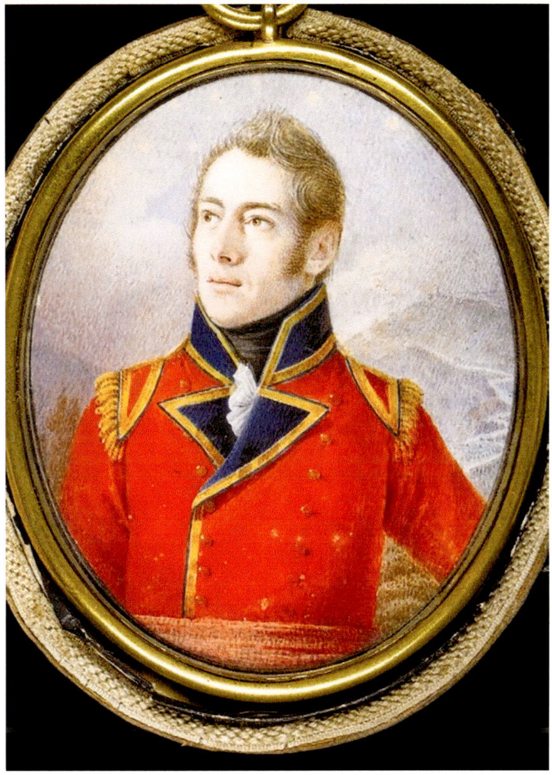

William Henry Milnes was the grandson of Richard Milnes, mentioned earlier. He was a career soldier, serving in the 1st Foot Guard throughout the Peninsular War. He was mortally wounded during the fighting at Hougoumont on 18 June 1815. He lies buried at Waterloo.

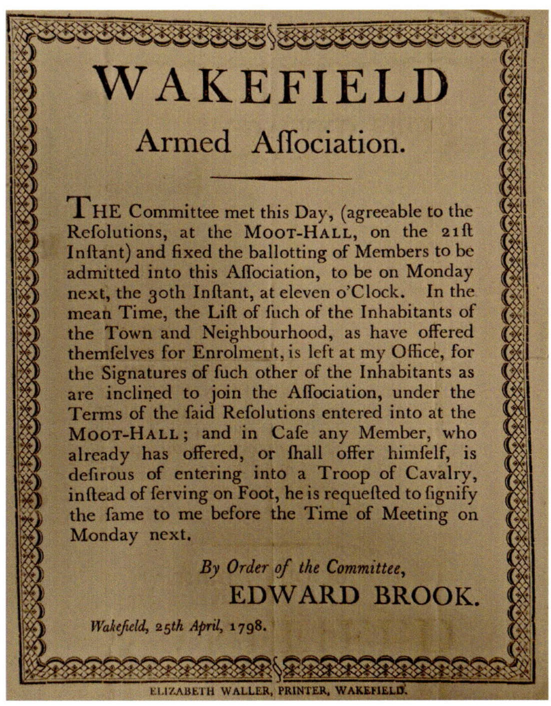

WAKEFIELD

Armed Aſſociation.

THE Committee met this Day, (agreeable to the Reſolutions, at the MOOT-HALL, on the 21ſt Inſtant) and fixed the ballotting of Members to be admitted into this Aſſociation, to be on Monday next, the 30th Inſtant, at eleven o'Clock. In the mean Time, the Liſt of ſuch of the Inhabitants of the Town and Neighbourhood, as have offered themſelves for Enrolment, is left at my Office, for the Signatures of ſuch other of the Inhabitants as are inclined to join the Aſſociation, under the Terms of the ſaid Reſolutions entered into at the MOOT-HALL; and in Caſe any Member, who already has offered, or ſhall offer himſelf, is deſirous of entering into a Troop of Cavalry, inſtead of ſerving on Foot, he is requeſted to ſignify the ſame to me before the Time of Meeting on Monday next.

By Order of the Committee,

EDWARD BROOK.

Wakefield, 25th April, 1798.

ELIZABETH WALLER, PRINTER, WAKEFIELD.

Recruiting poster for the Wakefield Armed Association – an early 'Dad's Army'.

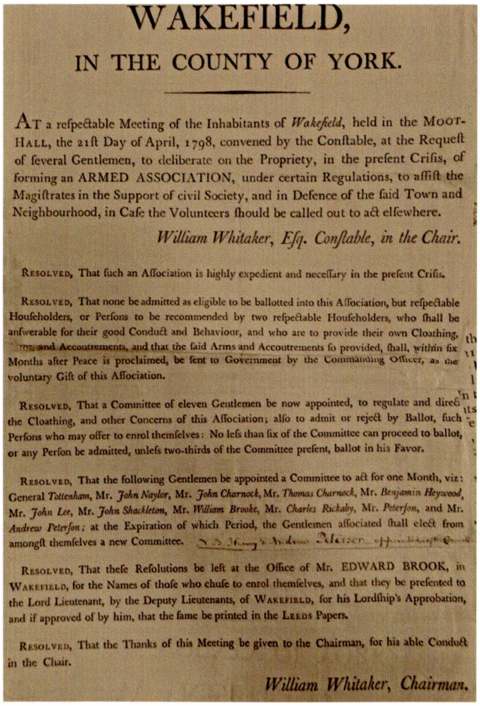

WAKEFIELD,

IN THE COUNTY OF YORK.

AT a reſpectable Meeting of the Inhabitants of *Wakefield*, held in the MOOT-HALL, the 21ſt Day of April, 1798, convened by the Conſtable, at the Requeſt of ſeveral Gentlemen, to deliberate on the Propriety, in the preſent Criſis, of forming an ARMED ASSOCIATION, under certain Regulations, to aſſiſt the Magiſtrates in the Support of civil Society, and in Defence of the ſaid Town and Neighbourhood, in Caſe the Volunteers ſhould be called out to act elſewhere.

William Whitaker, Eſq. Conſtable, in the Chair.

RESOLVED, That ſuch an Aſſociation is highly expedient and neceſſary in the preſent Criſis.

RESOLVED, That none be admitted as eligible to be ballotted into this Aſſociation, but reſpectable Houſeholders, or Perſons to be recommended by two reſpectable Houſeholders, who ſhall be anſwerable for their good Conduct and Behaviour, and who are to provide their own Cloathing, Arms and Accoutrements, and that the ſaid Arms and Accoutrements ſo provided, ſhall, within ſix Months after Peace is proclaimed, be ſent to Government by the Commanding Officer, as the voluntary Gift of this Aſſociation.

RESOLVED, That a Committee of eleven Gentlemen be now appointed, to regulate and direct the Cloathing, and other Concerns of this Aſſociation; alſo to admit or reject by Ballot, ſuch Perſons who may offer to enrol themſelves: No leſs than ſix of the Committee can proceed to ballot, or any Perſon be admitted, unleſs two-thirds of the Committee preſent, ballot in his Favor.

RESOLVED, That the following Gentlemen be appointed a Committee to act for one Month, viz: General *Tottenham*, Mr. *John Naylor*, Mr. *John Charnock*, Mr. *Thomas Charnock*, Mr. *Benjamin Heywood*, Mr. *John Lee*, Mr. *John Shackleton*, Mr. *William Brooke*, Mr. *Charles Rickaby*, Mr. *Peterſon*, and Mr. *Andrew Peterſon*; at the Expiration of which Period, the Gentlemen aſſociated ſhall elect from amongſt themſelves a new Committee.

RESOLVED, That theſe Reſolutions be left at the Office of Mr. EDWARD BROOK, in WAKEFIELD, for the Names of thoſe who chuſe to enrol themſelves, and that they be preſented to the Lord Lieutenant, by the Deputy Lieutenants, of WAKEFIELD, for his Lordſhip's Approbation, and if approved of by him, that the ſame be printed in the LEEDS Papers.

RESOLVED, That the Thanks of this Meeting be given to the Chairman, for his able Conduct in the Chair.

William Whitaker, Chairman.

List of officers of the Wakefield Armed Association from April 1798. The officers were the 'great and good' of the town.

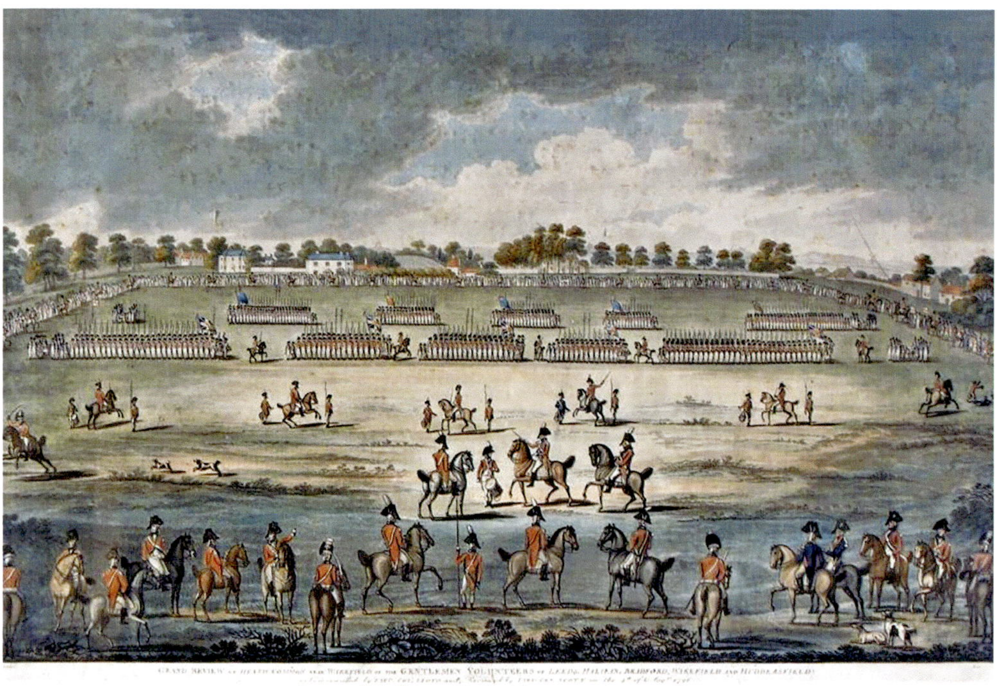

In 1795, Heath Common was the scene of a review of thousands of volunteers who had enlisted to fight for king and country. This marked the birth of what would later be the Territorial Army.

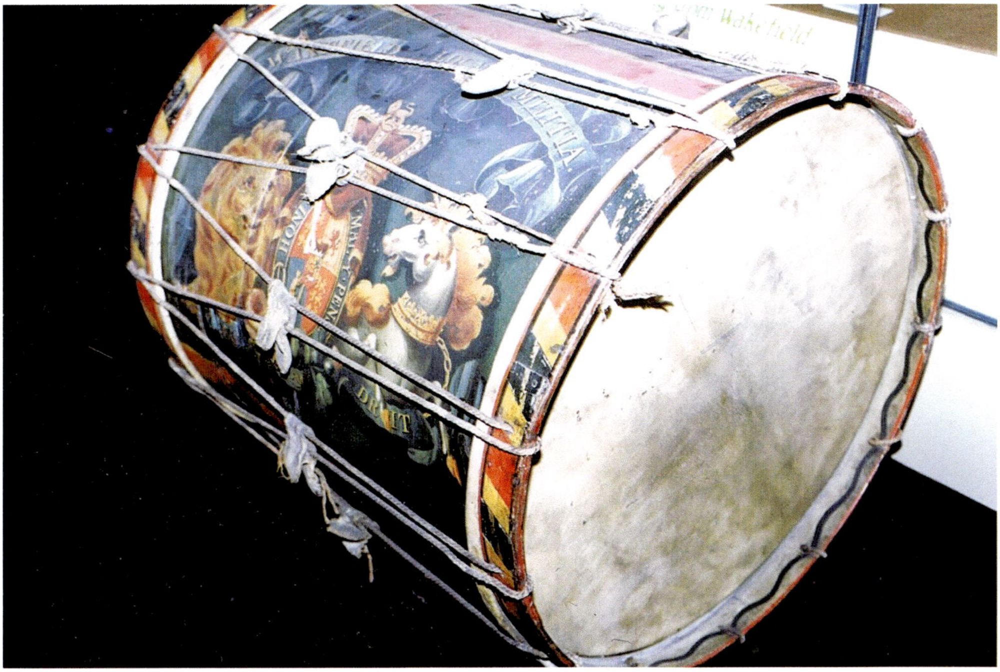

Drum of Wakefield Local Militia. Created in 1808 to replace the volunteers, the unit was called out to fight the Luddites in 1812. However, it was quickly found to contain Luddites and working-class radicals amongst the rank and file, and the Wakefield Local Militia were not delegated to combat Luddism. Instead, the Royal Wakefield Volunteers, raised from the middle- and upper-class men of the town, were mobilised and engaged the Luddites following the attack at Forster's Mill in Horbury.

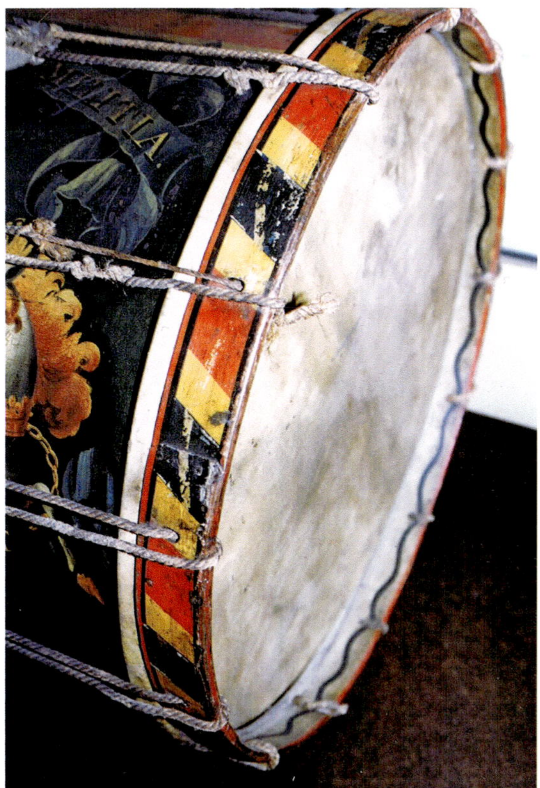

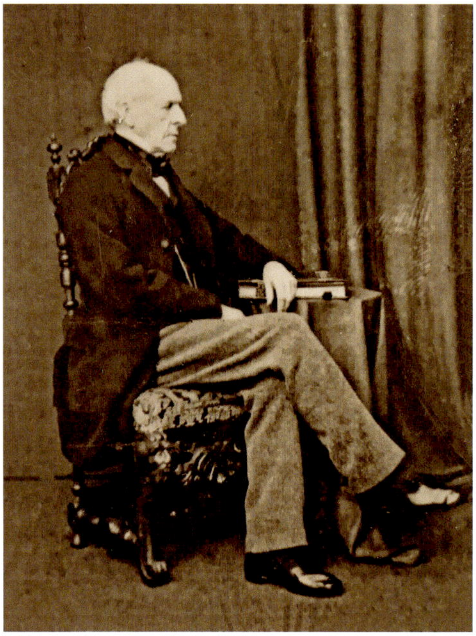

Daniel Gaskell, first MP for Wakefield, was an officer of the West Riding Yeomanry Cavalry between 1803 and 1812. This unit eventually became the Yorkshire Dragoons.

The volunteers disappeared for a generation. In the wake of the French campaign in Italy in 1859–60, Secretary of State for War Peel was convinced that France was hell bent on a war of European conquest and was planning to invade England. The nation was increasingly pro-German, and with Francophobic tendency running high with fears of a pan-European war breaking out, Peel put out a call for volunteers. By autumn 1859, 60,000 men had enrolled in new volunteer units and 171,000 had enrolled by the end of 1860. What would become the 4th Battalion King's Own Yorkshire Light Infantry was first organised as a battalion in November 1859 as the Wakefield Rifle Volunteers, and in the following year Wakefield and other nearby rifle volunteer companies were grouped as the 3rd Admin Battalion of Yorkshire West Riding Rifle Volunteers. Dressed in grey at first, in the French manner, in 1874 they were dressed in scarlet with blue facings. In 1880 the battalion was consolidated to form the 5th West Yorks Corps, which consisted of eleven companies.

The 5th became the 1st Volunteer Battalion KOYLI in 1883. During the Boer War they sent eight officers and 243 other ranks to serve with the regular troops in South Africa. Upon transfer to the Territorial Force in 1908, the 1st Volunteer Battalion was divided to form the regiment's 4th and 5th battalions, the former retaining the Wakefield headquarters. The KOYLI, and from 1968 the Light Infantry, were an important part of Wakefield for over 100 years. The George Street barracks became home to 299 Para Squadron, an army reserve unit that is part of 23 Para Engineer Regiment.

Wakefield men also volunteered to serve as soldiers of the queen. One was William Pickard, son of Richard Pickard and Elizabeth Britton of Beck Bottom. He was baptised on 2 October 1824. He enlisted in the 13th Light Dragoons at Hounslow on 16 October 1843 as Joseph Priestley and was made corporal 30 June 1846, then sergeant on 17 October 1852.

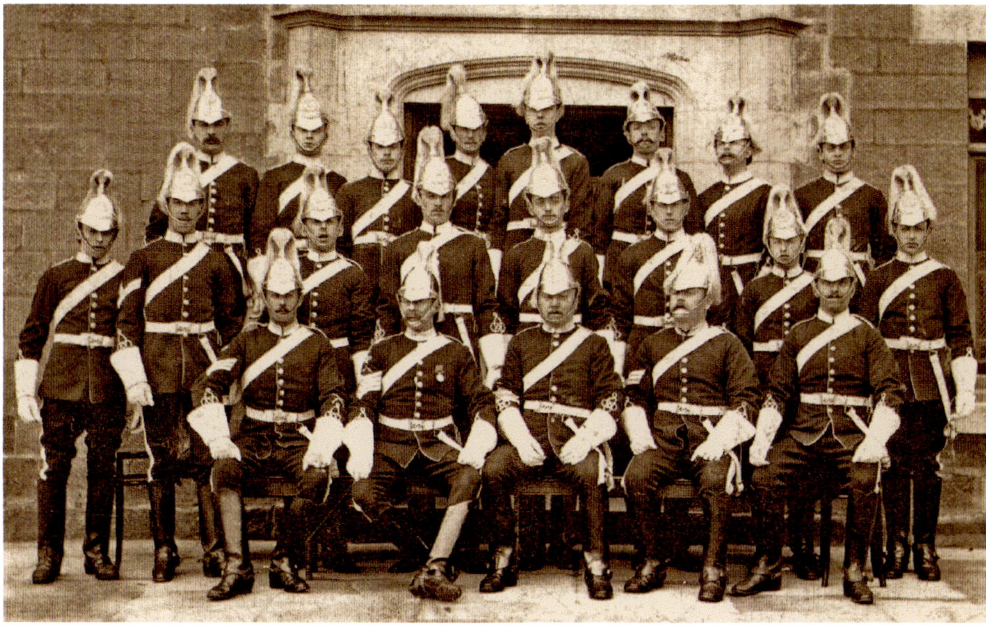

The Yorkshire Dragoons outside Heath Old Hall, *c.* 1880.

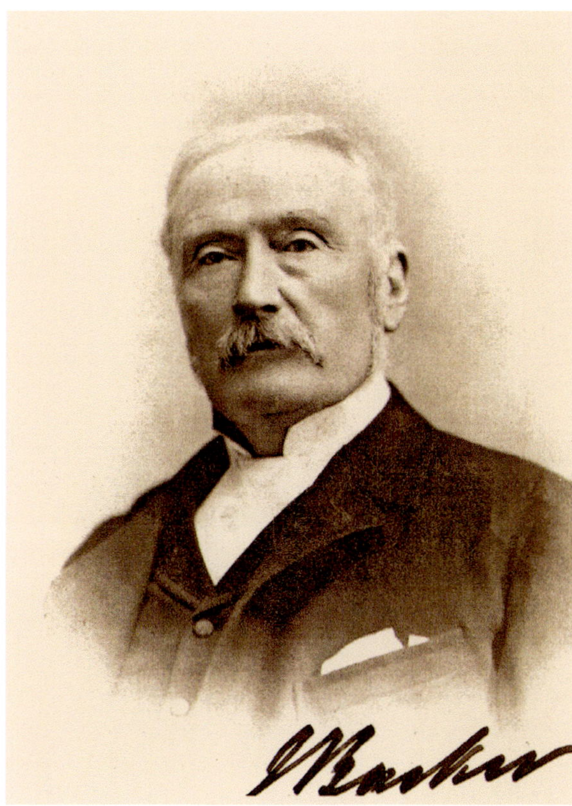

Major Joseph Barker, mill owner and senior officer of the Wakefield Rifle Volunteers.

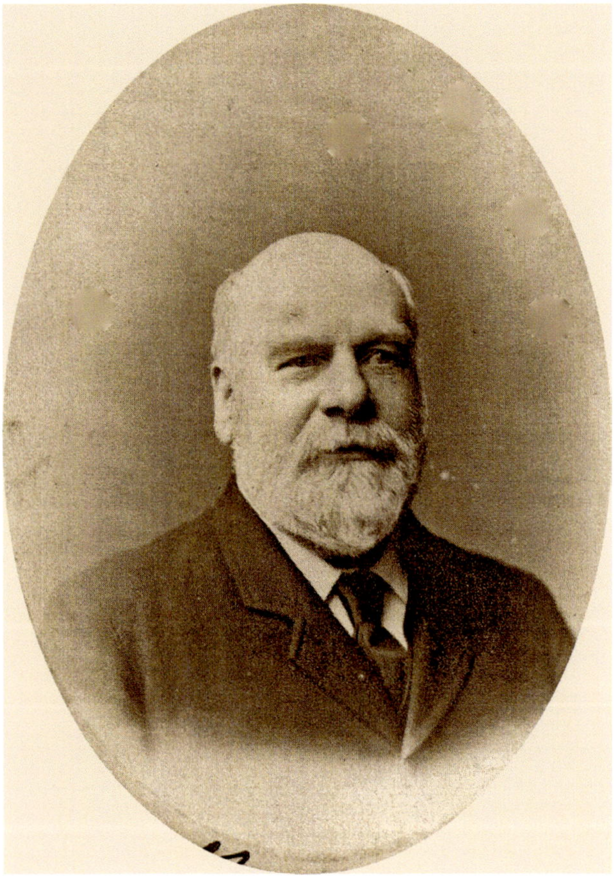

Colonel Edward Alexander MacKie of the Wakefield Rifle Volunteers. His sister, Edith Grace, paid for the rebuilding of St John's Parish Church in 1904.

With war against Russia declared, he travelled with the famous Light Brigade to the Crimea led by Lord Cardigan. The Light Brigade went into action on 19 September 1854 at Bulganak. By this time Priestley was acting as paymaster's clerk, meaning he was literate and, in theory, non-combatant. Whilst reconnoitring the Russia positions, his regiment came under Russian artillery fire. Captain Percy Smith reports:

> The shell that killed his horse must have missed me by a few inches. It hit his horse under the dock and burst at the same moment and the first thing I saw was the horse falling on its head with the belly so complete emptied out that I would see the joints of the spine. As the man was the Paymaster-Sergeant, he had no right to be under fire.

The shell also destroyed Priestley's left leg. He was the first British soldier wounded in the Crimea. Recovered from the battlefield, he was taken to the General Hospital at Scutari on 24 September. Sent home to England on 16 December 1854 aboard *The Talavera*, he landed at Chatham on 16 January 1855. In consequence of being permanently disabled, he was discharged on 2 October 1855 with a pension of 1*s* 8*d* per day. He was awarded the Crimean and Turkish medals and received the Distinguished Conduct medal for his actions at the Bulganak River. The medal came with an annuity of £20. In 1861, he married Emma Laxon in Norwich and was landlord of the Queen's Arms, Blackfriars Road, Yarmouth. Traumatised by the events in the Crimea, Priestley can be seen to have suffered from post-traumatic stress disorder. Unable to cope, he shot himself on 14 April 1871.

Another Crimean soldier, Private John Burgoyne, 23rd Regiment (Royal Welch Fusiliers), wrote to his father who was well known in the town:

> Inkerman, December 7th
>
> My Dear Father,
>
> After a Long delay I take up my pen. I will tell you all that has happened since I left England. After we landed in Turkey, we soon commenced our marching. We first went to Bulgaria, and there in the place we lost most of our brave men by sickness, but thank God I enjoyed very good health. After a long and painful stay we got on route to Russia when our men gave three hearty cheers. We landed in Russia (the Crimea), on the 18th Sept. quite safe. One the 19th our Regiment marched in front of the army with Sir George Brown at our head. At 12 o'clock we met the enemy but our appearance put them to flight, and they were pursued by our artillery, which gave them what they did not like. We lay there that night, and next morning we commenced our march. Sorry I am to say

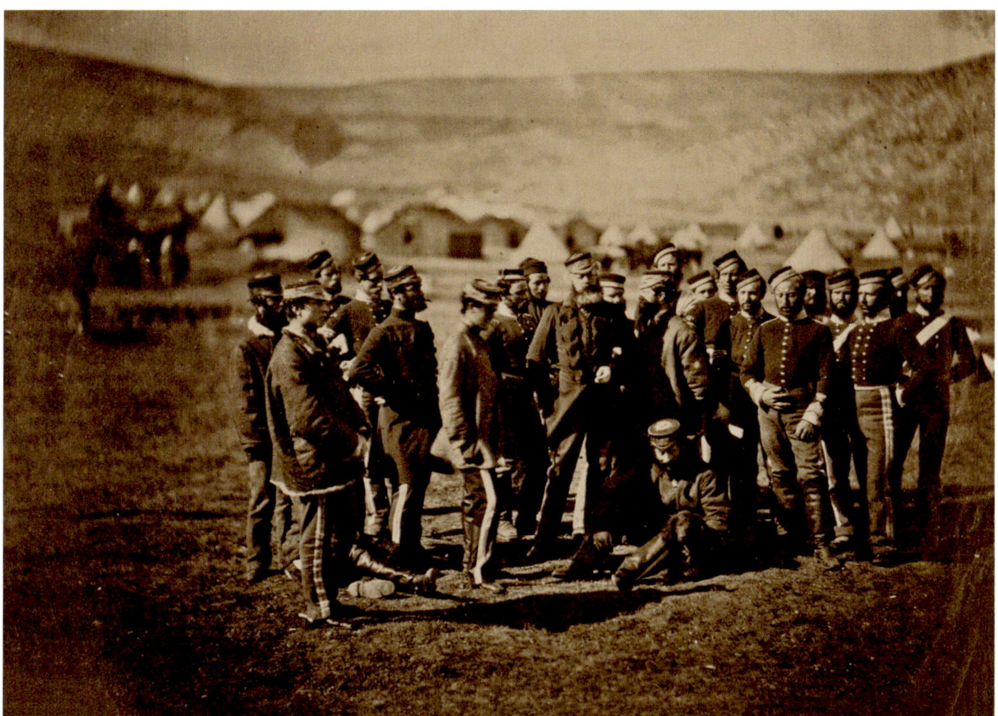

Officers of the 13th Light Dragoons in the Crimea during 1855. These men would have known the paymaster of the regiment, who hailed from Wakefield.

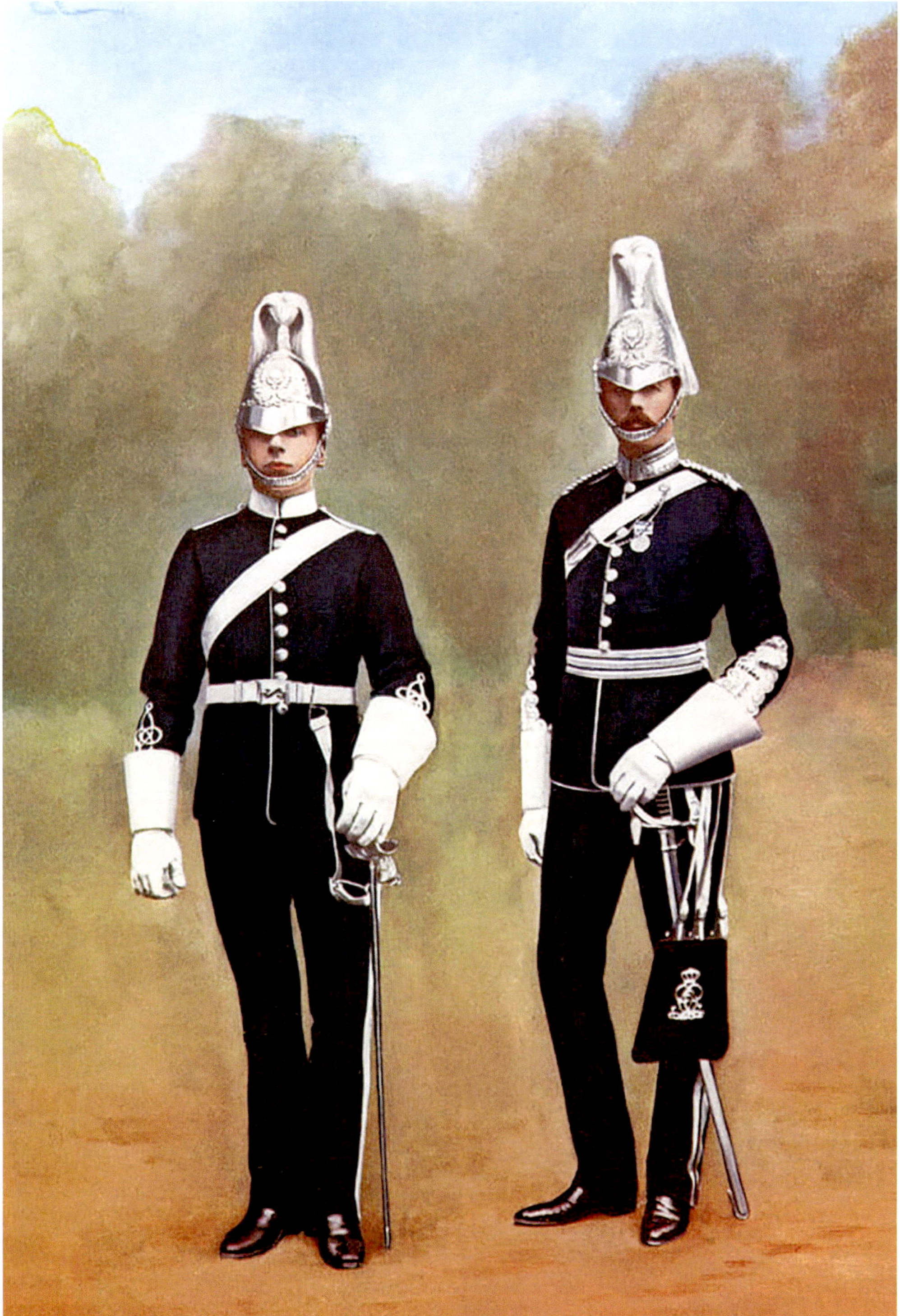

Officer and trooper of the Yorkshire Dragoons, *c.* 1900.

> it was the last march for many a poor fellow. At 12 o'clock we halted, and got orders to prepare for the enemy; General Saint Arnand [sic, Marshal Saint Arnaud] came with the news. We all rose and gave three cheers. At half-past one we met our foe mounted on the heights miles above our heads, their cannons pouring upon us, but we advanced coolly with General Brown at our head. He said – 'Now Royal Welsh, let them see what you can do!' We gained the day. Our army lost 1400 men. The poor 23rd suffered the most. We lost 210 killed and wounded. We buried the dead, and in a few days commenced our march again. We took a fort and 200 prisoners. At last we came in front of Sebastopol. It is a most beautiful place. We are hammering at it every day, but have not yet commenced work properly. On the 5th of November the Russians sallied out with 40,000 men. There was only about 200 of our regiment and about as many more of the 7th Regiment. They came on the high hills, and we were in a ravine. We kept them in play for three hours, until the French came up to our assistance, when we made a complete massacre of them. We took 400 prisoners, and the French took 9,000. We lost very few men, and 1 officer and 12 men made prisoners. If they would only let us go at them we would finish matters very soon. There have been several of the Russians have given themselves up to us, and they say that they are very badly off for provisions in Sebastopol. We are having winter clothing served out to us. It rains very much here. We have to engage every second night. We cannot tell the moment that we shall have to make a rush, but the Royal Welsh will do their duty, you may depend upon it.

Burgoyne was not alone in the 23rd; Private William Hamlet Floyd (2723) from Wakefield was also with the 23rd. He died of wounds aged twenty-nine on 26 May 1856. Private John Murray also served in the 23rd and was from Wakefield. Over sixty Wakefield men and boys fought in the Crimea (1854–56), and many never returned. Their names are not recorded on any memorial in the city.

6. The Twentieth Century

Wakefield men and women took up arms in the Boer War, First World War and Second World War. One heroine of the city was Nellie Spindler. Nellie was a staff nurse who was killed during the Battle of Passchendaele. She is one of only two British female casualties of the First World War buried in Belgium, and the only woman buried among more than 10,000 men at Lijssenthoek Military Cemetery. Spindler entered nursing in 1911 at the City Fever Hospital, Wakefield, and trained at Leeds Township Infirmary from 1912 to 1915. She joined the Queen Alexandra's Imperial Military Nursing Service (QAIMNS) in October 1915. In order to join it was necessary to be single or recently widowed, to have completed a three-year training course in a hospital approved by the War Office and to be over twenty-five years of age. Spindler, however, was only twenty-four at the time she signed up. On her application form, she said her year of birth was 1889 rather than 1891. It is possible that this was a mistake, but she may have concealed her true age so she would appear to be old enough to serve. After being accepted into the QAIMNS, from 10 November 1915 until 24 April 1917 she worked at Whittington Military Hospital, Lichfield. While there she was declared fit for service overseas. In May 1917, she travelled to France and worked in No. 2 General Hospital at Le Havre in the Somme before being transferred to No. 44 Casualty Clearing Station (CCS), which moved to Brandhoek, Belgium, in July 1917. Though about 3 miles from the front lines, Brandhoek was within range of the larger German guns, which, with its railway sidings and munitions dumps, was the target of frequent German shelling. On 21 August 1917, the CCS was bombarded, and at 11 a.m. Spindler was hit by an exploding shell along with four other nurses who were concussed. She died 20 minutes later in the arms of Sister Minnie Wood, the sister in charge. Her name is included in the memorial screens at York Minster's Five Sisters window. In 2018 a half-mile-long new road linking to Wakefield's new Eastern Relief Road in Stanley was named Nellie Spindler Drive following a public vote.

Gallipoli Remembered

Clement Bradley was born in Newmillerdam on 17 April 1895. He volunteered into the Royal Munster Fusiliers on 2 September 1914 along with a group of friends from the chapel. From working in Massie's draper shop on Marygate, he found himself posted to Gallipoli with the 7th Battalion:

> On June 9th 1915 we started by train from Basingstoke to Liverpool. Arriving at Liverpool we boarded S.S. Mauretania, and once on-board active service started. I must say that it was 11.15 when our battalion got on board and settled into our different bunks on E Deck. By 2.15, before the boat left dock, we were on guard.

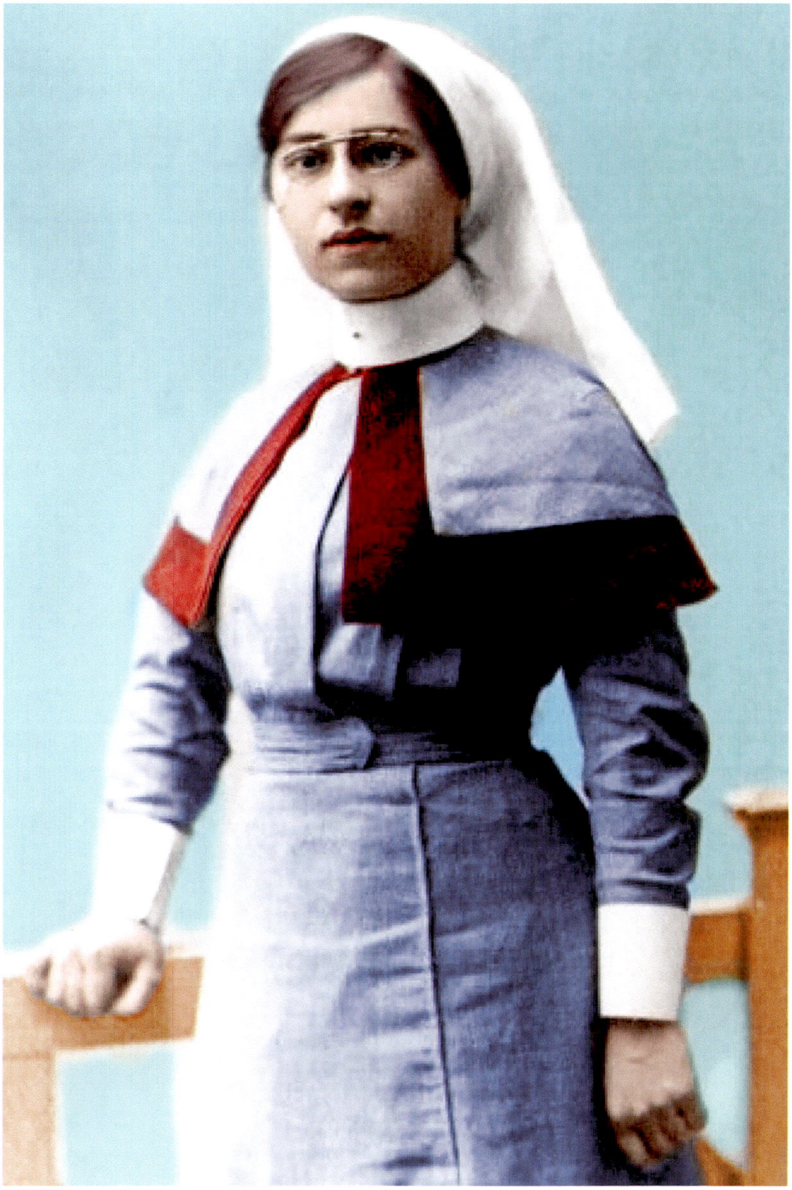

Nellie Spindler, one of Wakefield's most notable heroines.

I have no doubt you will wonder what we were doing guard for on board. Well, the duty of the guard was to be always on the look-out for submarines. Of course, there was no need to look for those in dock. At 5 p.m. she loosed her moorings, and we were at once unlinked from England – some of us never to return. Everything was in splendid going order by bed time that night, but at dawn the next morning we sighted a submarine, but, being guarded by three destroyers, we were really safe, so it came to the lot of our battalion to signal the sight of the first submarine to the three destroyers. I must say we all thought it a red tape idea doing guard on board ship, but after that incident we

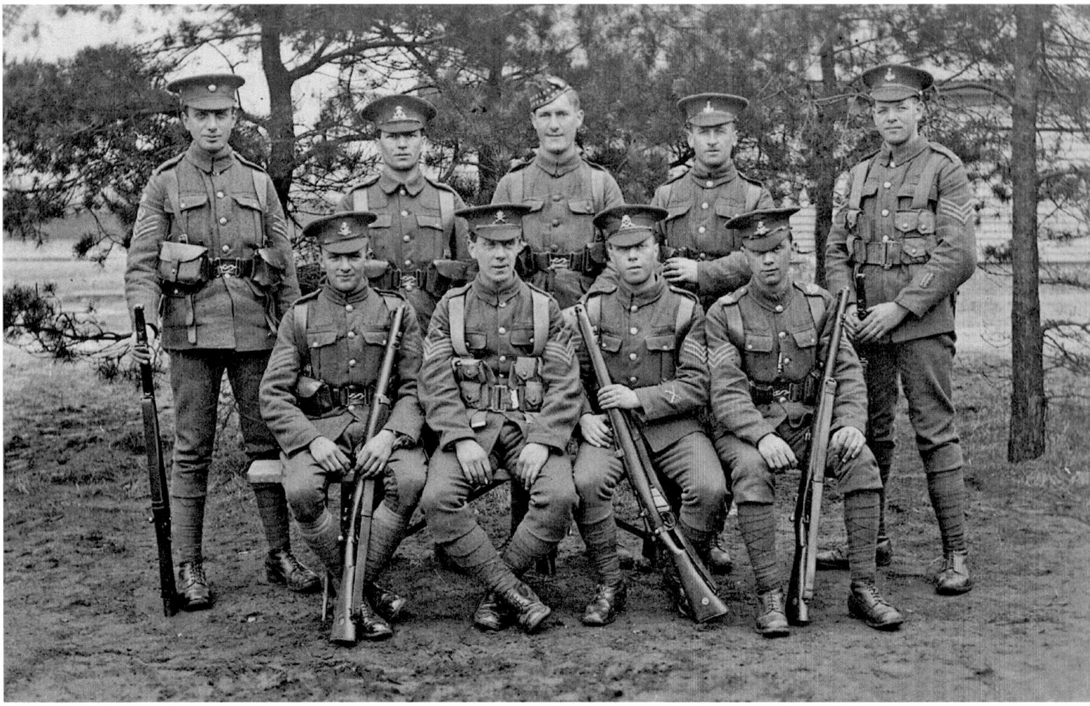

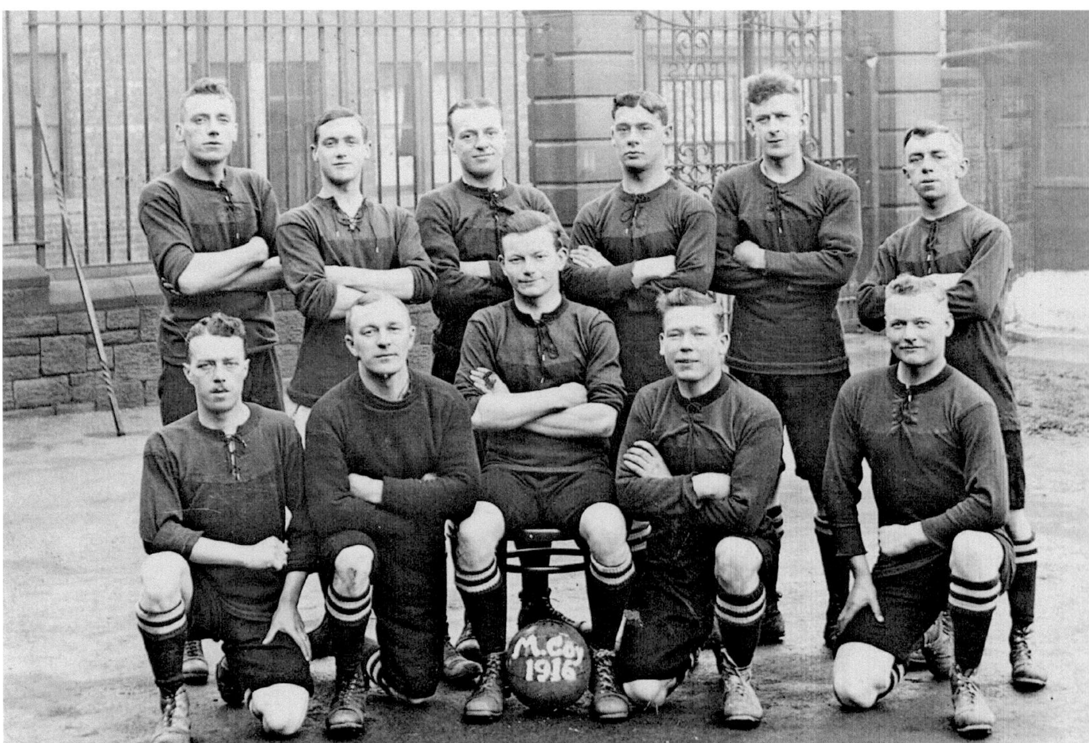
M. Coy
1916

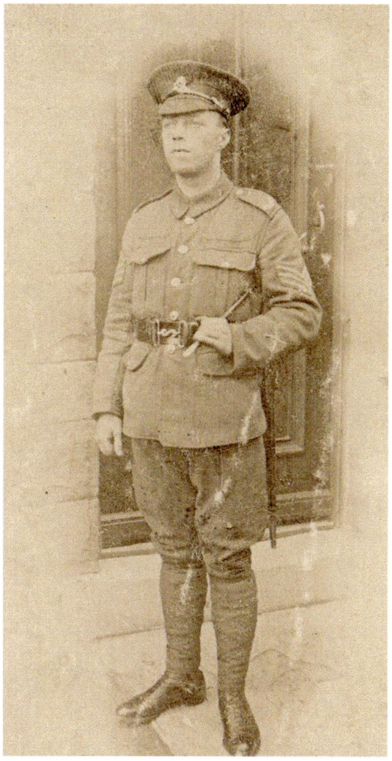

Right and previous page: Charles Henry Drake, co-founder of Wakefield-based Drake & Warters, was a professional solider. Enlisting in 1913, he served in the Staffordshire regiment. Wounded to the head in November 1914, he spent the remainder of the war on home service, responsible for training.

were quite content to skim the blue waters all day, looking for any sign of danger....After stopping at Gibraltar about half-an-hour – every boat has to stop there for orders of some kind – we continued our journey through the beautiful Mediterranean Sea.

Our next encounter was just off the south of Greece, about 80 miles from our destination (Lemnos). It was dusk, and we were ordered to have every light out on the ship, as we were in a very dangerous zone. We were certainly chased, as we had to go full speed ahead all the night, and when the morning came we found ourselves just entering the harbour at Mudros, which is a part of Lemnos Island...I shall never forget it. It was scorching hot, as had been the last few days, and there we were, with nothing but a bottle full of water and plenty of biscuits and bully.

After stopping on Lemnos for three weeks unloading stores, Clement found himself heading to Gallipoli and combat:

Not having been in active service before, we were all quite excited and could not get on to the transport ship (which was to take us to the danger zone) quick enough. However, once all on board we were anxious to know how long we should be before we were off, and we were soon to find out, as it was about 4 o'clock in the afternoon before we had all got on board, and it was a dull time waiting for her to sail, as we were packed like herrings in a box. We could not walk about, there was no room.

At last dusk came, and we found ourselves really on the war-path. About 7 hours' sail brought us into Suvla Bay, and it was still dark. Very silently we were again put in smaller boats. After all the boats had been filled we all pulled for the shore, which was about two miles off. We had to keep about two hundred yards apart. In a very short time we were about 500 yards from that awful rocky beach, and that is where the fun started. At 400 yards we got ping, ping, ping. That was our baptism of fire.

They came quicker and quicker and then, bang, and a shell would drop about 20 yards away. There was nothing for us to do now but to jump into the water, which everybody did, some never to get out again. I must say I know now what it is to have your blood boiling, as we all were very hot stuff just then. At last, after struggling in the water, we got on to the rocks, and my word, wasn't it hot. Turks were here, there and everywhere. But though only lads, all of us, the wary Turks ran for their lives as we flew at them with bayonets fixed ... We continued advancing, and we very soon had a mile to our credit, and by the end of the first day, from 4 a.m. to 7 p.m. we had 1½ to our credit. When dusk came and we had to dig ourselves in, I can tell you there was no sleep, as it was ping, ping, bang, bang all the night through. However, the next morning, without having any food, off we were again, and by the end of the third day we were three miles from the shore. The third night was most awful, especially the roll-call. Out of 1,000 there were only 400 of us left...That night was the first chance for something to eat, but I, being a stretcher-bearer, had not even that chance, as you could still hear our wounded comrades calling for help, so off we went. That was three days' continual work, but the third night was our first chance of sleep and rest, and I can tell you I just laid down in the gully on the rough ground and went fast asleep.

The fighting for the next five days was very little – no advancing etc. At the end of the eighth day, I had only had one meal, which consisted of rice pudding made of water, rice and sugar (fine) and bully-beef and biscuits boiled in a kind of broth. The ninth, and the fatal day with me, came. It was a beautiful day, the sun shining, lovely. We had got the order to advance at 12 and it was about 10.30 so I was busy filling the water bottles for any wounded. At five minutes to twelve I was waiting for the signal to advance and it came, and you should have seen our boys go – not half. We, being the stretcher-bearers, had to advance 500 yards behind the front line. This we were doing when, just as I and a comrade were running with a stretcher to the aid of the column, there came a crack just by my side. It was so sudden that I did not know it was me. I found myself lying full length on the ground and when I looked at my leg it was a sight. The pain was too intense to feel much. I sat up to have a better view of it, and to pull off my boot and puttie, when ping, ping, two bullets came through my hat and I had to lay down quite still for two hours, as the snipers had got me fixed.

After three days in no-man's land without water, food or shelter, Clement was eventually picked off the battlefield, made safe and taken to:

...the 1st Stationary Australian Hospital, and there I stayed for five weeks, and I must say I had a fairly happy time. At the end of the fifth week the Aquitania came into the harbour at Mudros on her maiden voyage as a hospital ship, so I was put on board for England.

I cannot explain how glad I was when once she set sail for home, sweet home, on the return voyage, which was seven days. We called at Naples and I had the opportunity of looking at Mount Vesuvius and beautiful Italy.

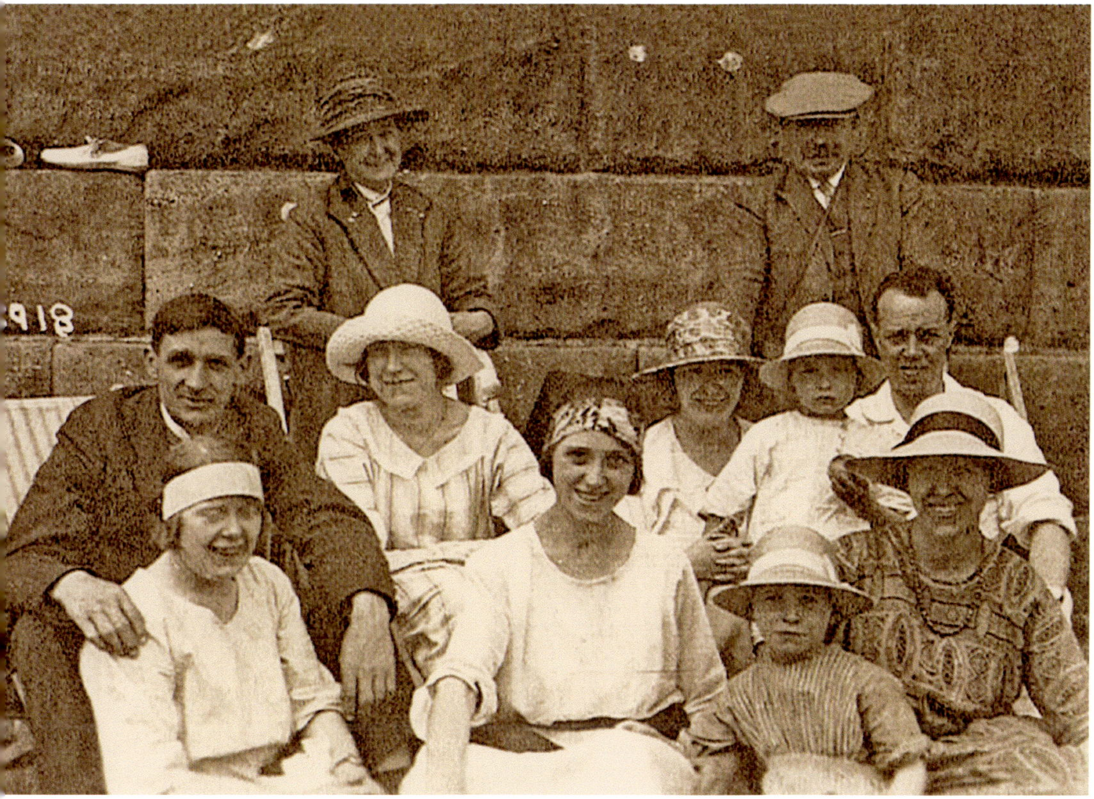

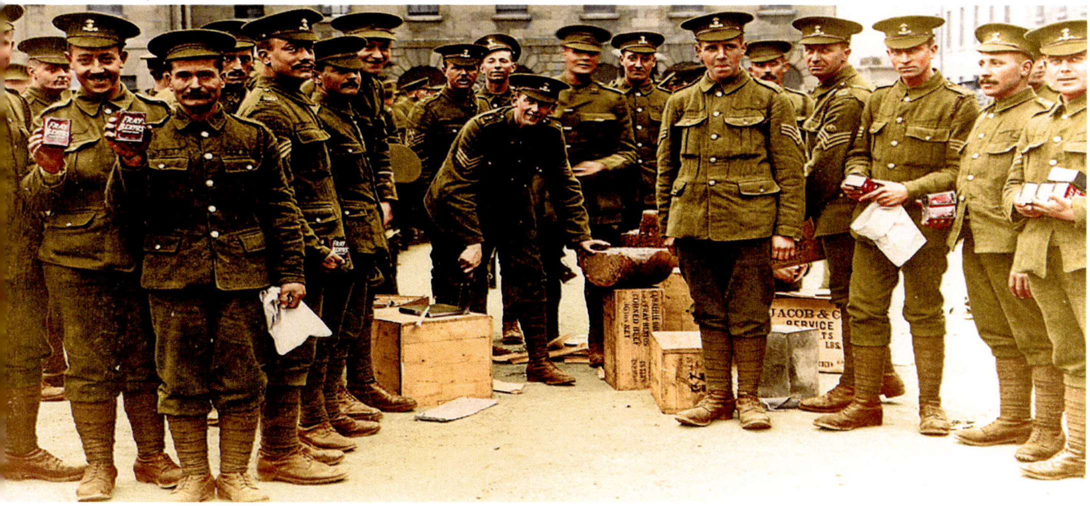

Above images and next page top: Clement Bradley (seated extreme left) was a Wakefield man. He enlisted in the Royal Munster Fusiliers and found himself posted to Gallipoli, where he was severely wounded. On the extreme right, seated in the second row, is his brother-in-law Charles Henry Drake. In front is Lilly Drake, and sat on her father's knee is the author's grandmother, Jean Drake.

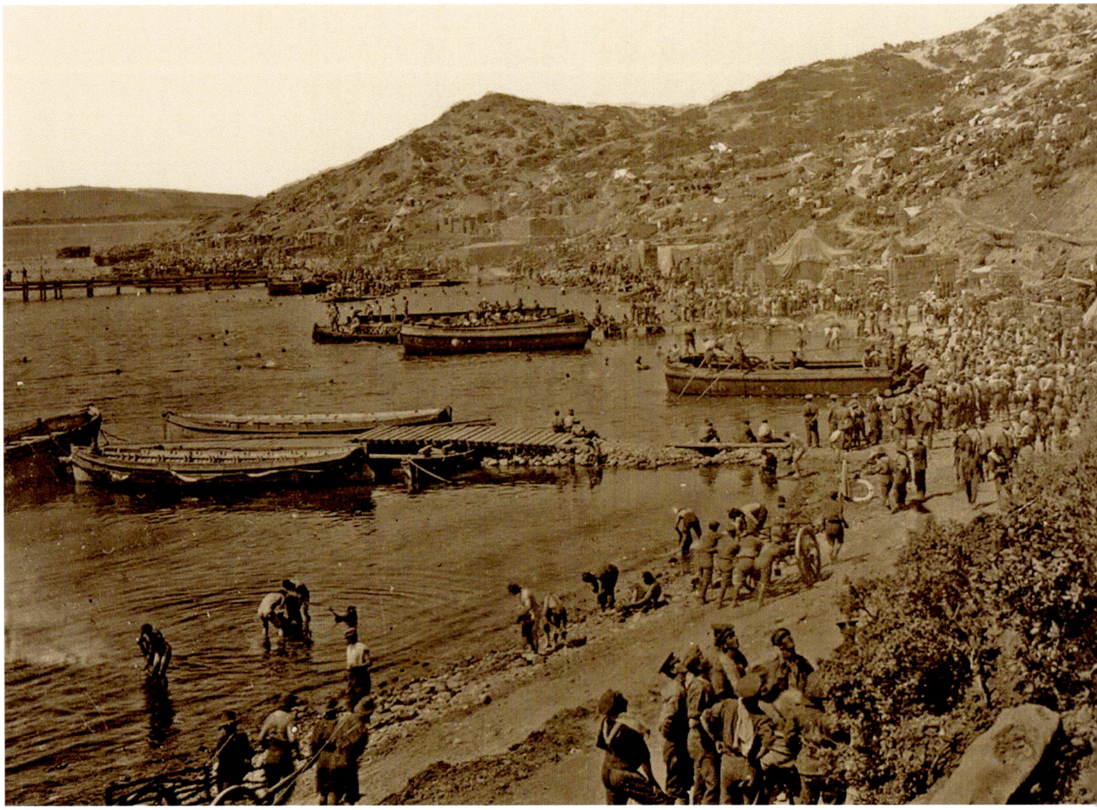

Once in hospital, his left leg was amputated above the knee after gangrene had set in. He was given a cork leg. A keen motorbike rider, he often used his leg as a handy place to store tools by pushing them into the cork, much to the horror of onlookers. As his letter alludes to, he and his wider family – the Harvey clan – attended Westgate End Chapel. Clement died in 1972. He married Mary Bradley in 1919. Their son Eric became an officer on the staff in India during the Second World War and their second son, known as 'Big Jim', was captured in Burma in March 1942 and held captive by the Japanese in unspeakable conditions. A cousin was amongst the first to liberate Bergen-Belsen, and had to threaten to shoot his own men to stop them feeding the inmates.

Wings Over Italy

Dennis 'Gus' Varey was born on 5 March 1922, son of John Varey and Nelly Harvey. Educated at Thornes House Boys' School and then Silcoates, as war was declared he was working in Ossett for the Prudential. The bombing of Wakefield on 5 March 1941 fell close to his home on the Lupset estate and close to family living on Horbury Road:

> The call up age for the armed forces was 21, however they would take volunteers at the age of 18 years. On reaching 19 I decided to volunteer. I was the last of the Harvey boys to go. I was told to report to the RAF volunteer reserve station in Huddersfield with

> about a dozen other lads, where we were given a test in English and Maths. I then had an interview with a Warrant Officer and was told that I would be accepted to be trained as aircrew. I officially joined the RAF on 27 November 1941. At the end of December 1941, I was passed as Air Observer and co-pilot. I was aircrafts man 2nd class.
>
> Then we were taken to the station to catch a train to the RAF training camp at Padgate near Warrington, Lancashire. I was one member of an intake of raw recruits, completing induction forms, followed by a thorough medical examination and intelligence testing.

After basic training he volunteered for – and passed – air crew selection. He was placed into the British Commonwealth Air Training Plan and travelled abord RMS *Rangitiki* to South Africa, then to his posting at Hillside, Bulawayo, in Southern Rhodesia, learning to fly on Tiger Moths and American Harvards. Training continued in Egypt on Harvards and Kittyhawks. Put on leave in Palestine, he visited Jerusalem and Gaza. Returning to Egypt, he flew across the pyramids before being posted to Libya. From Libya, Naples was the next stopping point in December 1943. It had taken him two years to train to be a pilot. In April 1944 he was posted to 260 Squadron, which had become operational in October 1940 in the north of Scotland flying a mix of air defence and convoy patrols. In April 1941 the squadron was withdrawn to prepare to move overseas, and in August it reached Egypt. The squadron had fought at El Alamein, the invasion of Sicily and Italy. He joined 260 at Cutella on the Adriatic coast at the start of May. It was here that on arriving Dennis was told the squadron already had a Dennis (Flight Sergeant Dennis Copping, who was reported missing 28 June 1942) and was told he would have to use a different name. For reasons lost to time, he chose the name Gus.

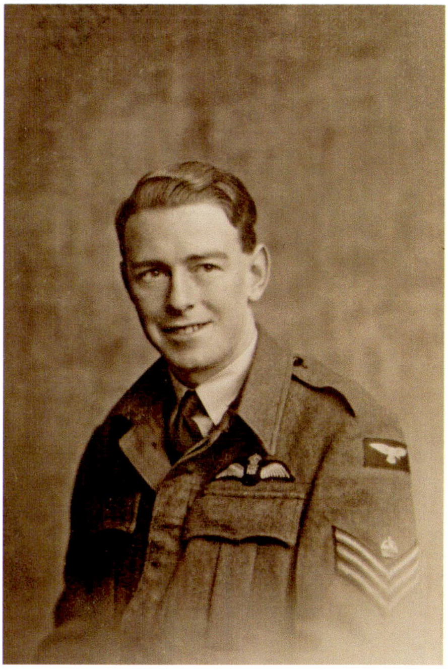

Dennis Varey (1922–2007).

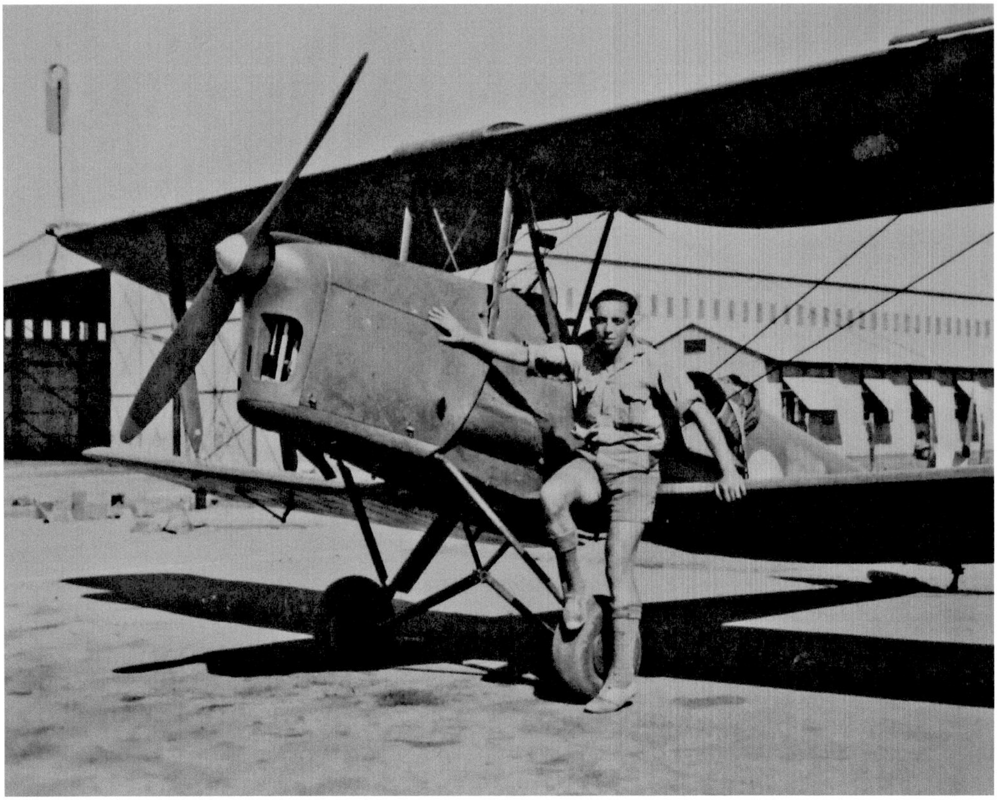

Learning to fly, Bulawayo, 1942.

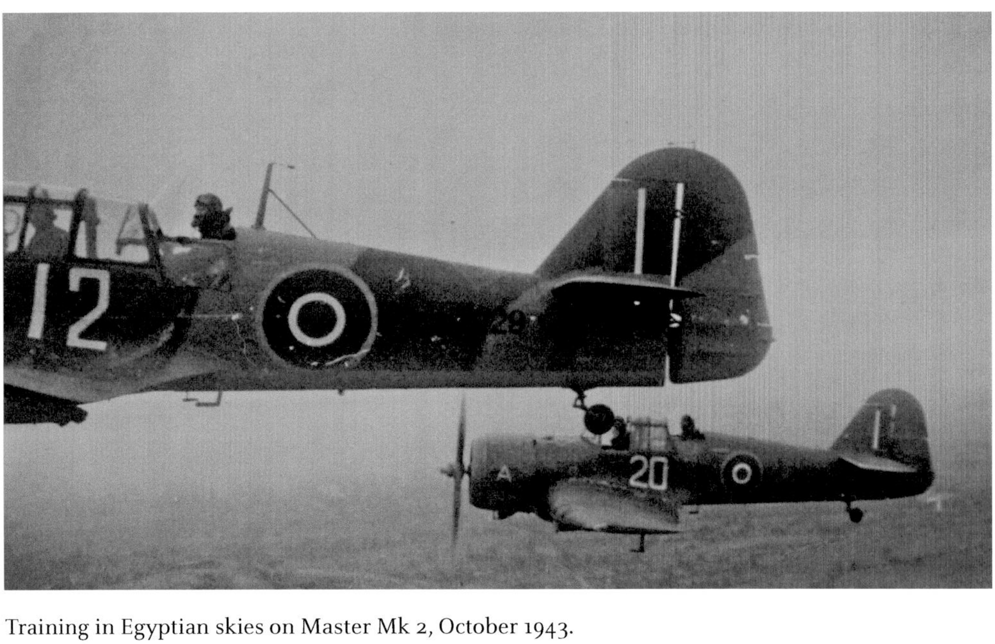

Training in Egyptian skies on Master Mk 2, October 1943.

One of Dennis's friends was the squadron's intelligence officer, who became an international star – Christopher Lee. Rather than separating officers and NCOs, all the pilots and squadron staff messed together. The mess during the Egyptian campaign had been kept well stocked with beer and other luxuries thanks to a 'borrowed' German Heinkel HE111 Bomber called *Delta Lilly*. In Italy, veteran pilot Lionel Shepherd was keen to keep the standards up, so Dennis and close friend Mervyn Talbot obtained a Ford 8-tonne light van and used to trade NAAFI rations with Italian farmers – on one memorable trip they brought back a cow, several chickens and geese.

It was not all fun and games in Italy. The 260 was a dive bomber squadron and equipped with P51 Mustangs. Dennis flew over Monte Cassino in the attacks on the Hitler and Gothic lines, as well as the invasion of the south of France known as Operation Dragoon. As ground attack, 260 was involved in supporting the infantry, as Dennis explains:

> We could be on stand by for 60 or 30 minute take off waiting for targets from Rover. In other cases, once we were in the air, on a Recce, an army forward observation post called a 'Rover' gave us clear directions as to our target, sometimes laying down a smoke marker for us. These directions were given to us on the radio. Quite often there would be several Squadrons in the same area at the same time and the 'Rover' control would call us in consecutively. Mostly if we were not Cab Ranking that we day, we were briefed about the op before we went up and given a series of pre-defined targets in scale of importance if the primary target was obscured.
>
> In the morning, our intelligence officer, in this case Chris or to give his proper name Pilot Officer C P Lee, gave us a briefing as to the role which we were to play in support of the PBI. It was up to us to provide close support to the troops on the ground, clearing a way for them to advance past mortars, heavy guns etc. We either attacked pre-assigned targets, or went on armed recces to pre-arranged target zones that had been requested by the infantry by Rover David control. Facing flak was, in the scheme of things, no worse than the PBI being mortared or shelled every day, and slogging up muddy mountains in torrential rain to be mown down by German MG fire. We gave them the support they needed to clear the Jerries out. We were trying to fight a war in Italy without adequate support, and tried to overcome this with air superiority and artillery.

On 23 August whilst bombing German positions around Bologna, his Mustang HS-D was hit by German Flak. He was wounded to the arm by splinters from a 20-mm cannon shell. Coaxing his battered aircraft back to base whilst loosing blood, he was taken to the military hospital and patched up. He returned to duty in late summer 1944, suffering from 'battle fatigue'. Unable to fly combat operations, he acted as understudy to the intelligence officer, the aforementioned Chris Lee. Dennis completed his tour of operations at the end of November 1944 – the chance of surviving a tour of 200 hours was less than 50 per cent – and he found himself posted to a training squadron for the remainder of the war.

> I posted in April RAF Holme on Spalding Moor, flying Hurricanes. I was teaching night fighter pilots how to defend bombing wings. Not as fast on the level as the Mustang, the Hurricane performed well in the roll assigned for them. I was here for most of April, and

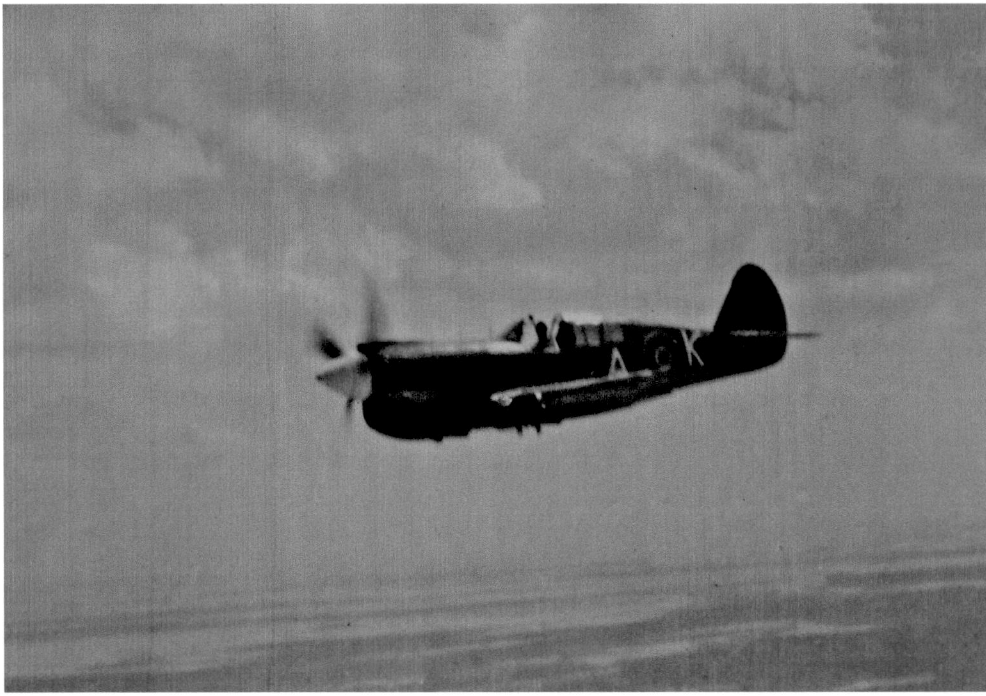

Dive bombing training aboard the P40 Kittyhawk.

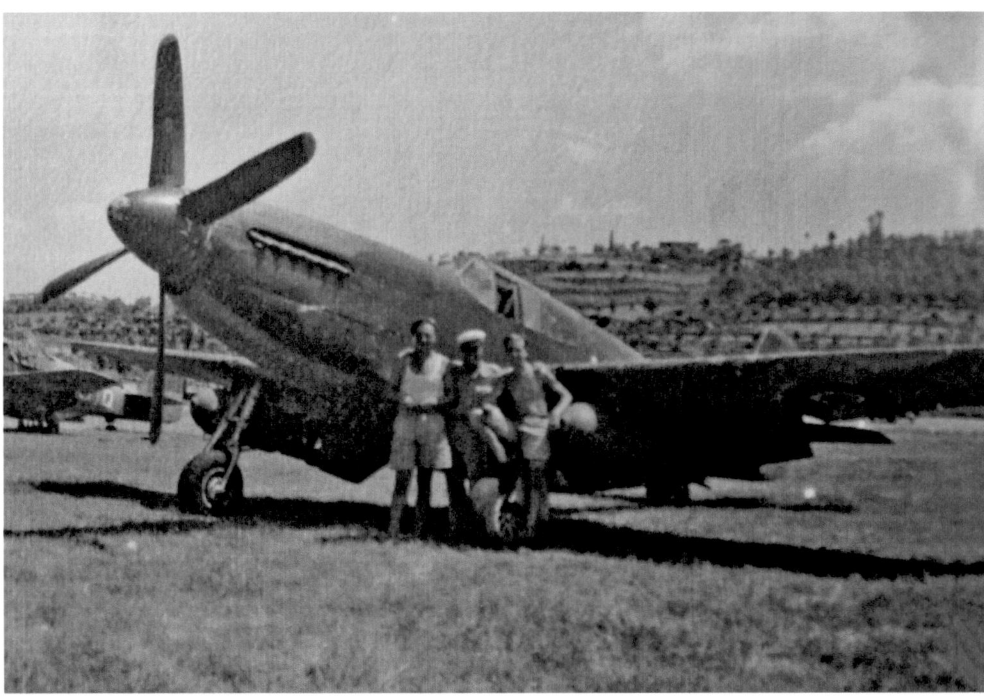

P-51 Mustang HS-D, Dennis Varey's aircraft on 260 Squadron.

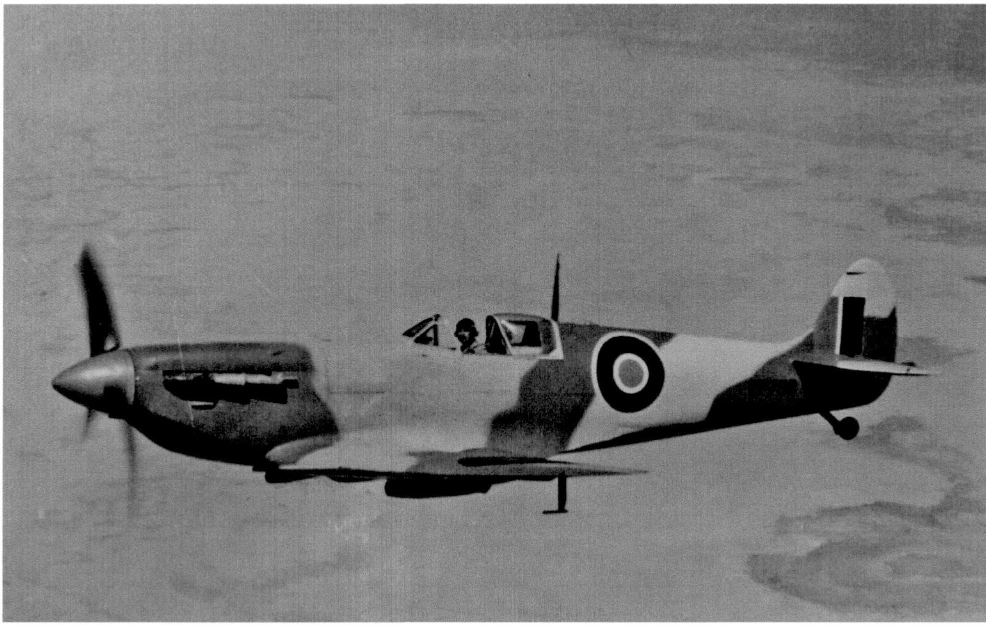

Dennis flying his spitfire at RAF Rednal, summer 1945.

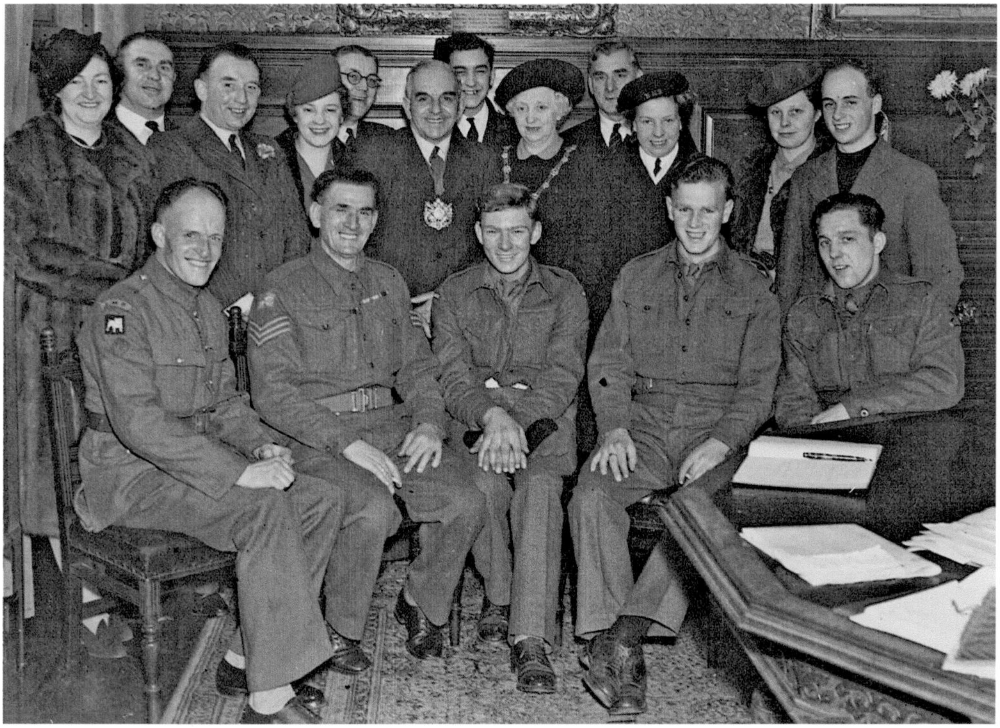

The mayor of Wakefield with some local war veterans as part of the fundraising event 'Wakefield Salutes the Soldier' on 3–16 June 1942.

> in May, it was off to 1660 Operational Conversion Unit, at Swinderby until October '45. Again, we had Spits and Hurricanes. I was given this ancient Hurricane to fly, but once I was up it had a total electrics failure and I had a prang, pancaking onto the Lincolnshire farm land … Having flown both the Mk 2 Hurricane and Mk5 Spitfires, the Hurricane was a better gun platform: it was more stable, and packed a bigger punch when armed with cannons. It could take damage the Spitfire could not. The Mustang outclassed them both. It was the best single engine fighter of the war. I ended flying the Mosquito. It really was a marvellous plane to fly: best aircraft I ever flew.

The 260 Squadron was disbanded on 19 August 1945. Demobbed in 1947 with the rank of Warrant Officer 1st Class, 'Gus' passed away in 2007, having suffered from prostate cancer for many years. For a little boy, being sat on my uncle's knee as he smoked his pipe and told his tales, this was the real-life Biggles.

Bletchley Park Remembers

As well as soldiers, sailors and airmen, the armed forces need 'eyes and ears' for intelligence. During the Second World War the 'eyes and ears' were Bletchley Park, which, as Dr P. Judkins' research notes, the history of which is now well publicised in both print and film. The story of Bletchley though is continually changing and being added to, as documents that are no longer classified come into the public domain for study. One such document added to the National Archives in 2019 recorded the involvement of Barbara Annie Dixon at Bletchley. She was involved in the translation of messages that had been

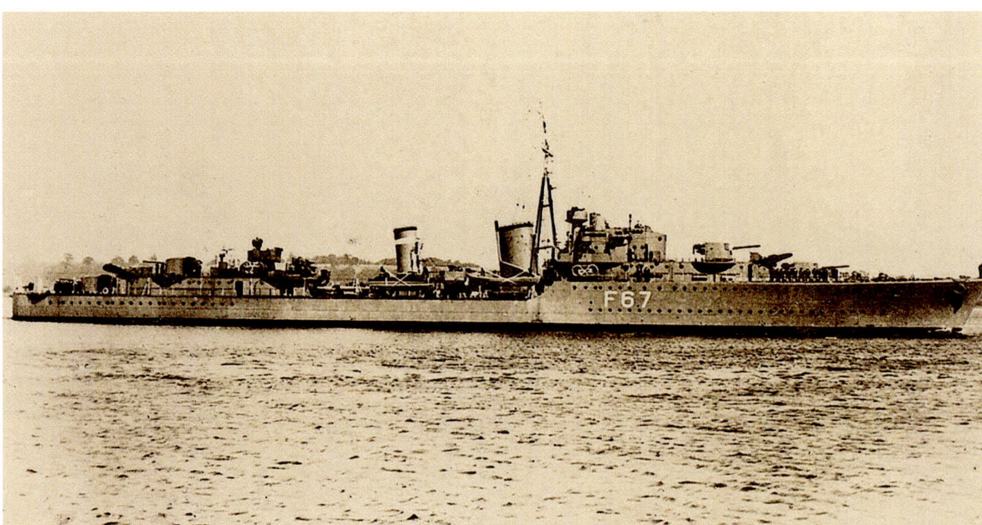

As well as 'salute the soldier', there were many other drives to commit money towards weapons. One, Warship Week in the Wakefield area, earned enough to purchase a destroyer and HMS *Bedouin* was associated with Wakefield as a result. HMS *Bedouin* had a distinguished career before being sunk in June 1942 while leading an attack of British destroyers against a superior force of Italian cruisers during a convoy to resupply the island of Malta.

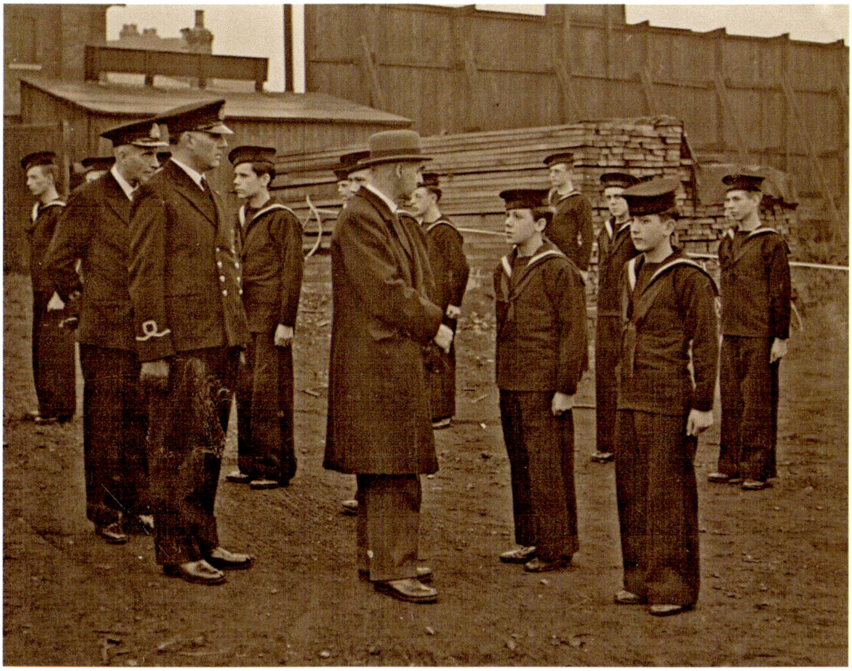

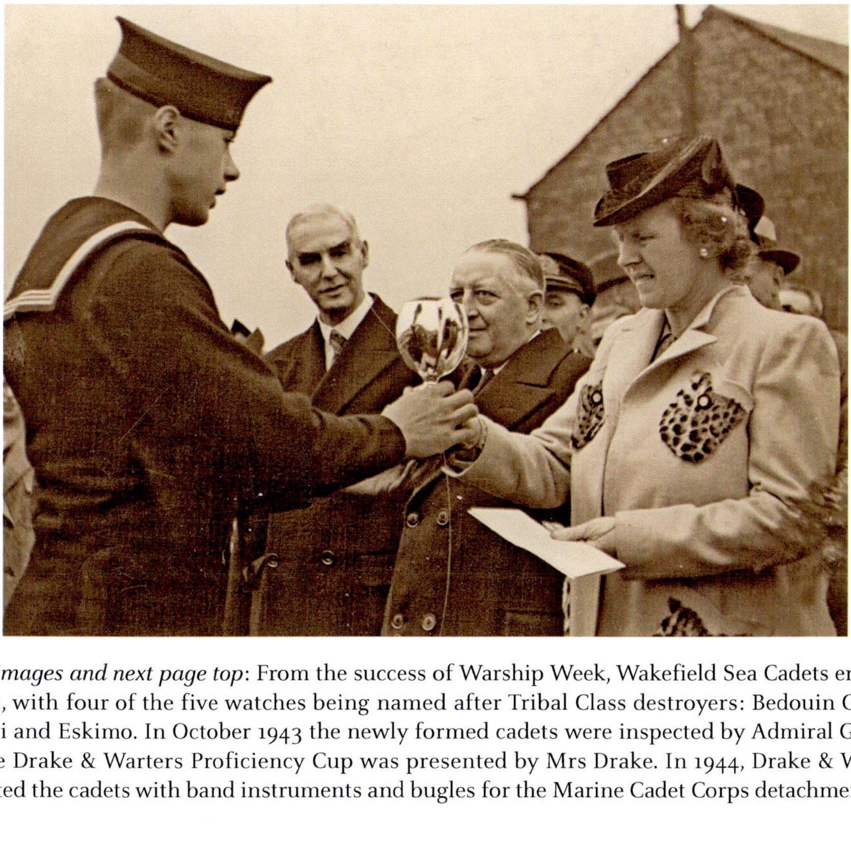

Above images and next page top: From the success of Warship Week, Wakefield Sea Cadets emerged in 1943, with four of the five watches being named after Tribal Class destroyers: Bedouin Gurkha, Ashanti and Eskimo. In October 1943 the newly formed cadets were inspected by Admiral Gunson, and the Drake & Warters Proficiency Cup was presented by Mrs Drake. In 1944, Drake & Warters presented the cadets with band instruments and bugles for the Marine Cadet Corps detachment.

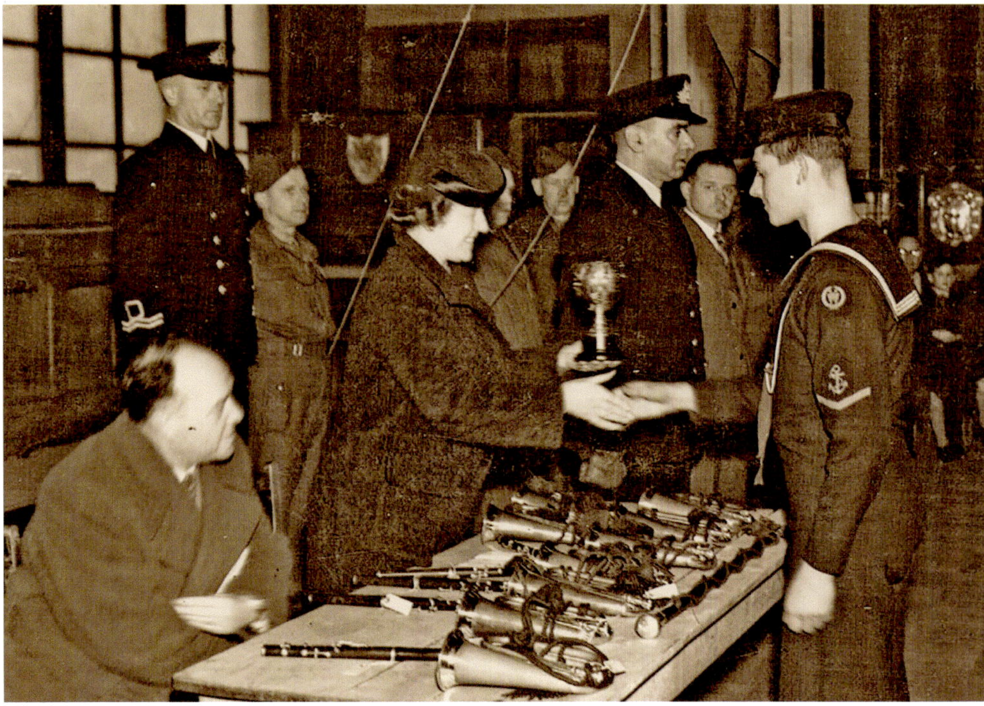

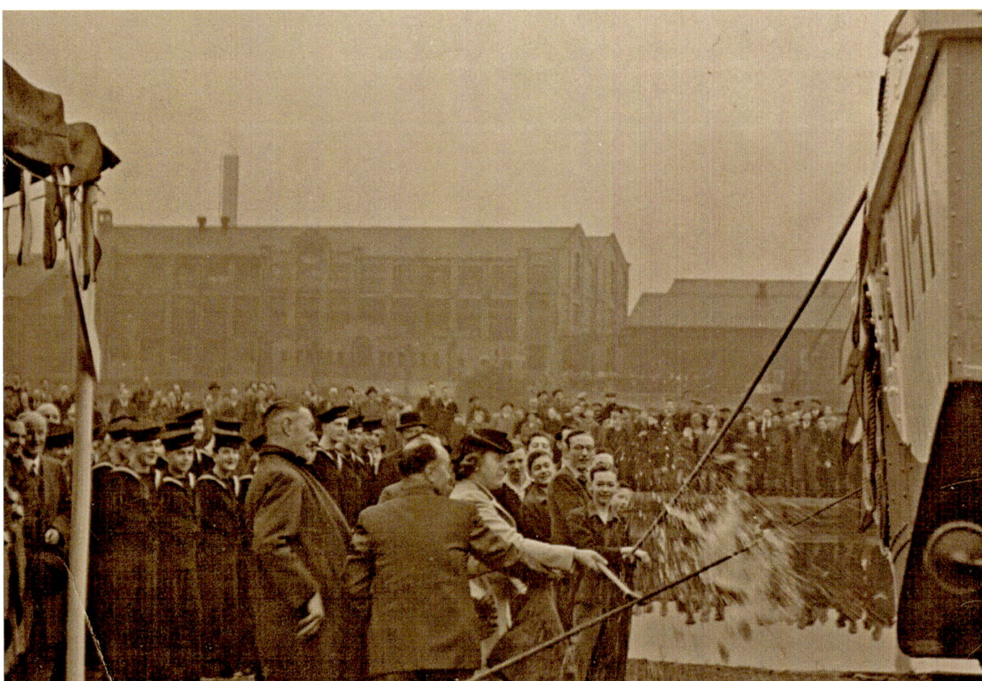

During the Second World War, Drake & Warters built seventy-two landing craft assault, which were used during the D-Day landings. Here we see the launch of the first, on 13 October 1943.

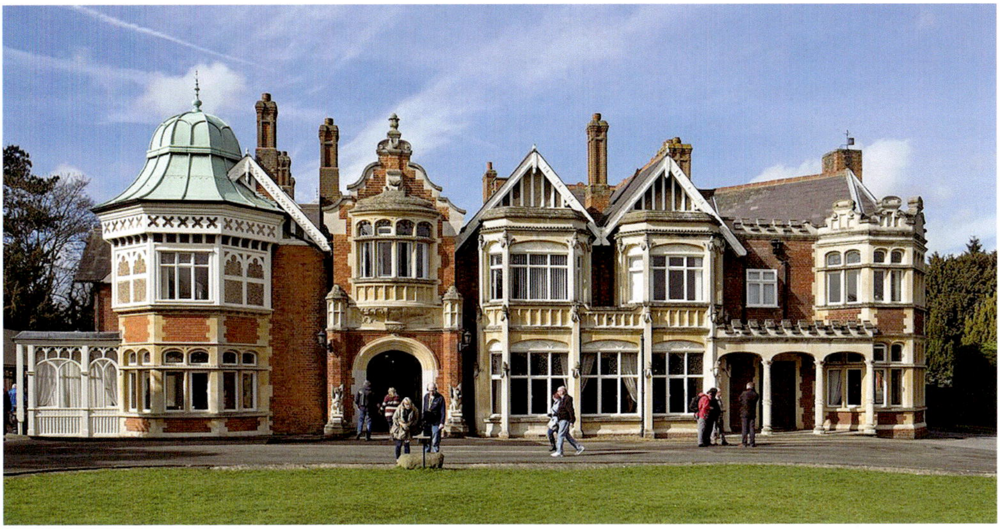

Bletchley Park was where well-known Wakefield resident Barbara Perraudin, née Dixon worked as a code breaker.

decoded from intercepts of German messages transmitted using the Enigma machine at the time when the V1 and V2 missiles were being developed. The intercepted messages were written in highly technical German and relied upon expert translators to understand the contents. Her work was vital to identify the routes the missiles took to launch sites, the date and times of the launch and the path of the rockets. Because of Barabara's work in providing vital intelligence, many missiles were destroyed before reaching their targets and saved countless hundreds of lives. Barbara Dixon had been well known to many interested in Wakefield's history. She married Ray Perraudin, an early president of Wakefield Civic Society. She never spoke of her wartime role.

The Dambusters

During the Second World War, thousands of men from across the district were called up and, like Barbara, played a key part in the Allied victory. Operation Chastise (the attack on German dams carried out on the night of 16/17 May 1943 by 617 Squadron RAF Bomber Command), more commonly known as the Dambusters Raid, involved men from Wakefield and district. Sergeant Wilfred Ibbotson (rear gunner on ED887 AJ-A) was born in Netherton and was lost on the return flight from the raid, where they attacked the Möhne Reservoir. Flight Sergeant William Hatton (flight engineer on ED906 AJ-J), born in Wakefield, attacked the Möhne Reservoir and returned safely, though sadly lost his life on 14 September 1943. Another was Pilot Officer Cyril Anderson (promoted to pilot officer on 16 April 1943, gazetted June 1943; pilot ED924 AJ-Y), born in Wakefield. His primary target was Diemel Dam, but he was redirected to the Sorpe Dam. Flak damage to his rear guns made them unserviceable. With fog and mist on route at 3.15 and unable to pinpoint the Sorpe Dam, they returned to Scampton. They all now rest in Rheinberg Commonwealth War Graves Cemetery. These men's stories are true of many of hundreds of others.

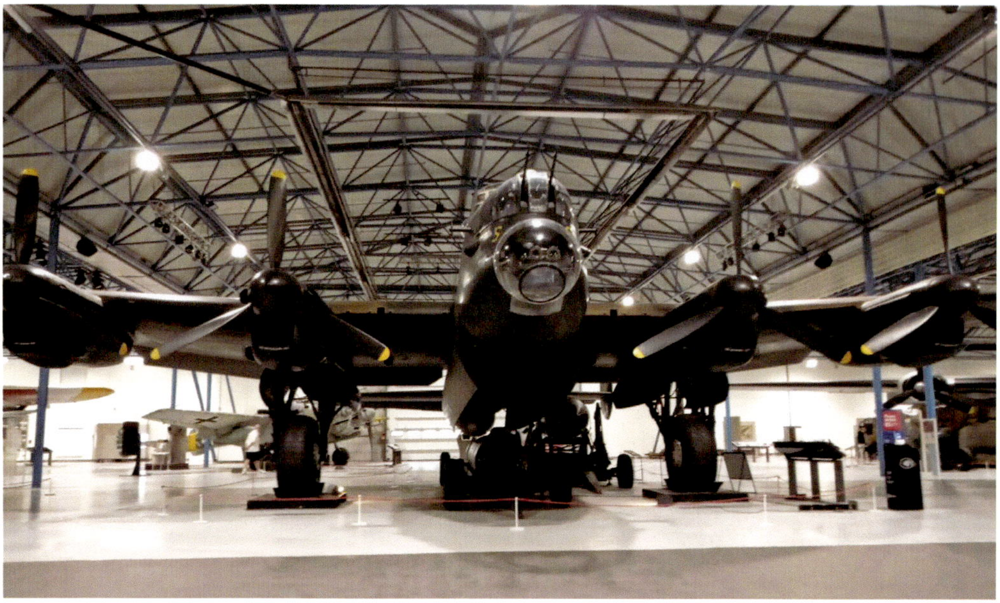

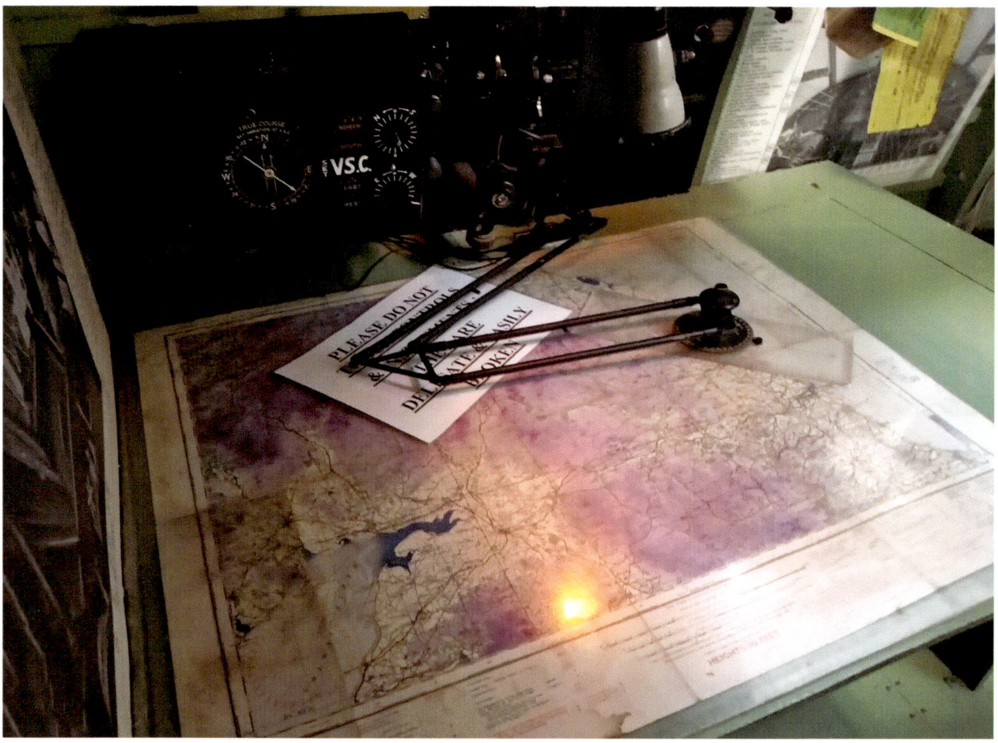

This spread page and next spread page: Perhaps the most iconic of all aircraft from the Second World War is the Lancaster. These magnificent aeroplanes were well known by Wakefield men, such as Pilot Officer Cyril Anderson, one of many local lads called up to Bomber Command. Your author was given the opportunity to climb aboard a Lancaster at Hendon RAF Museum.

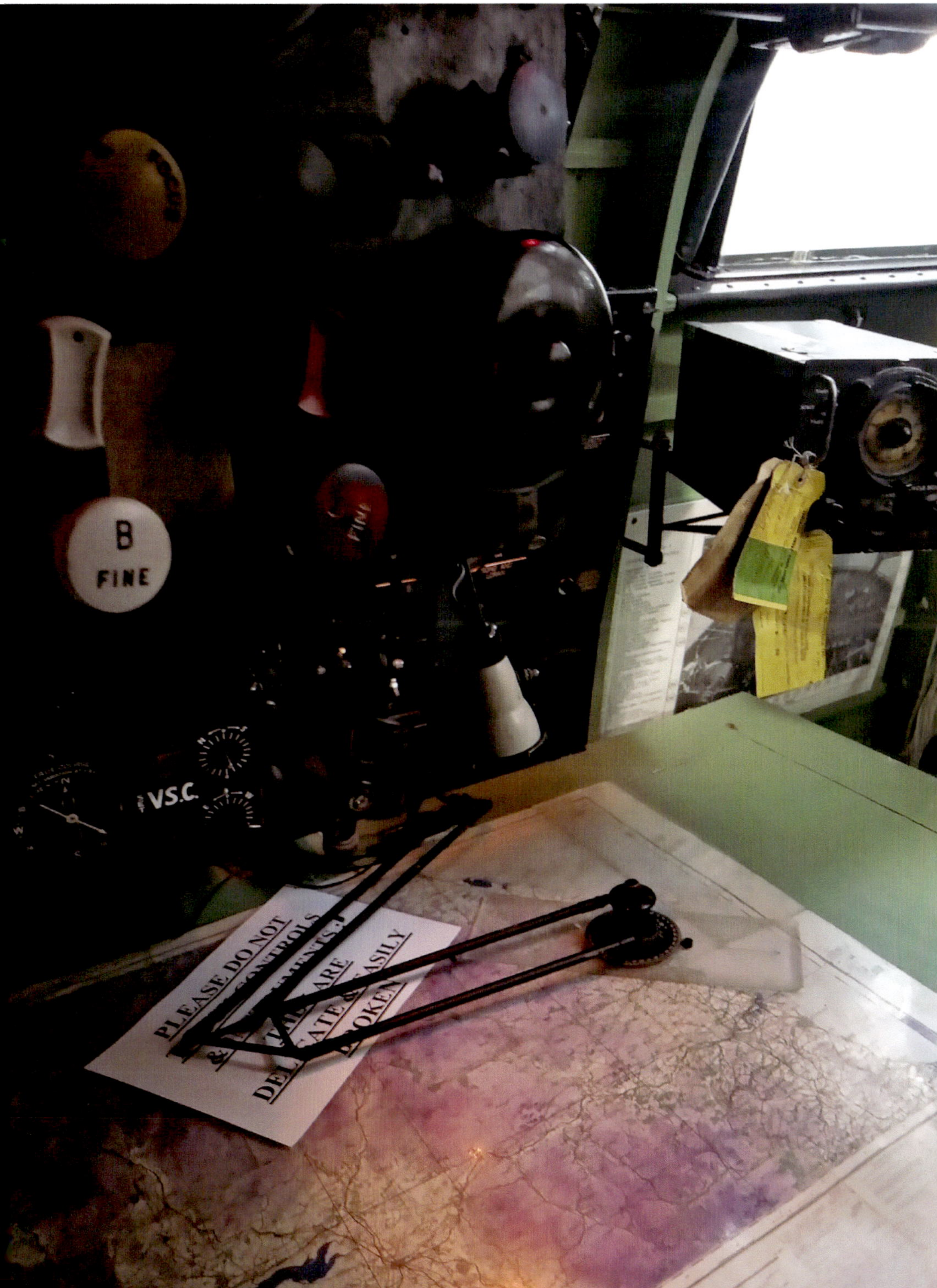
B
FINE
VS.C.
PLEASE DO NOT

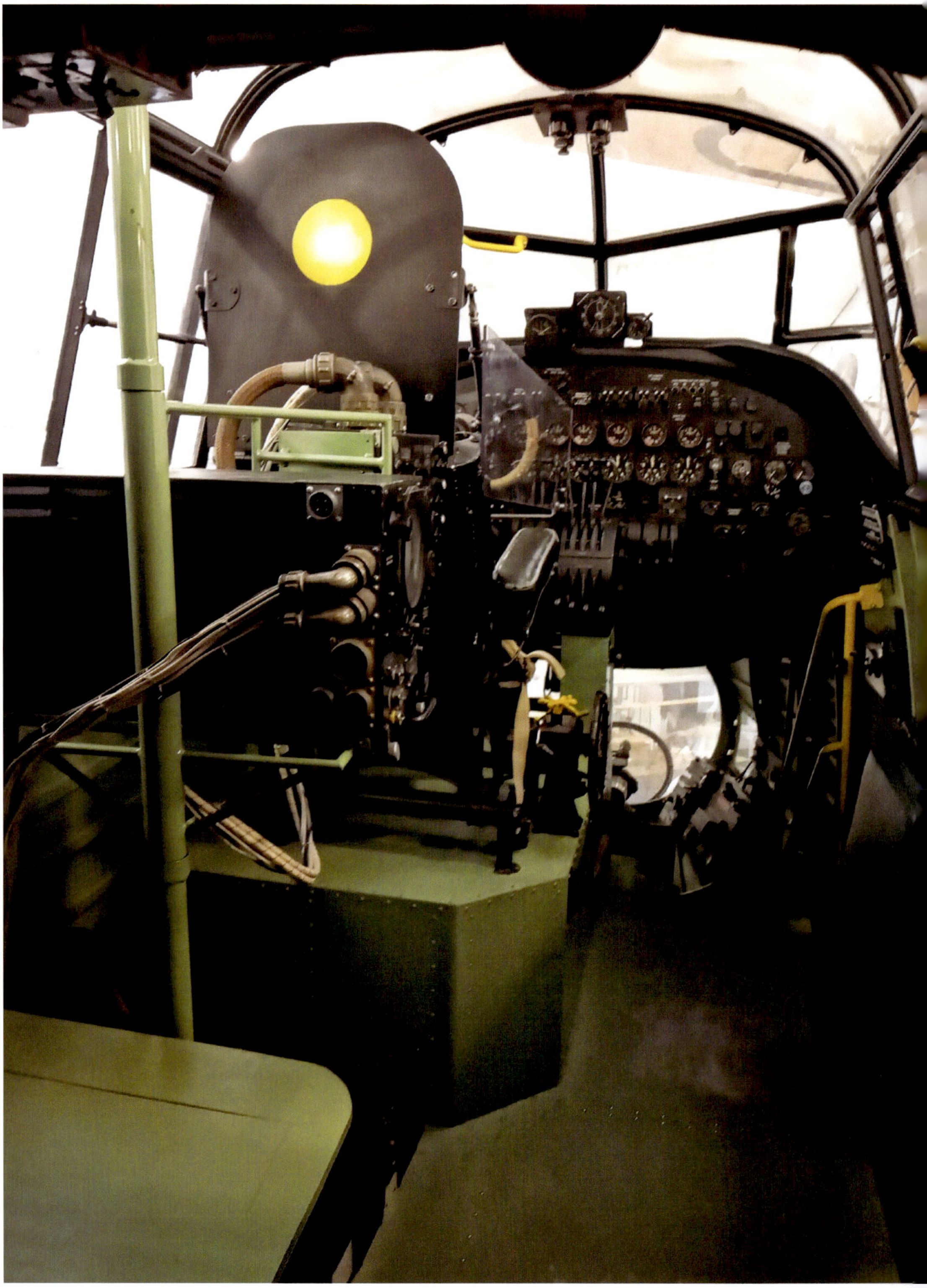

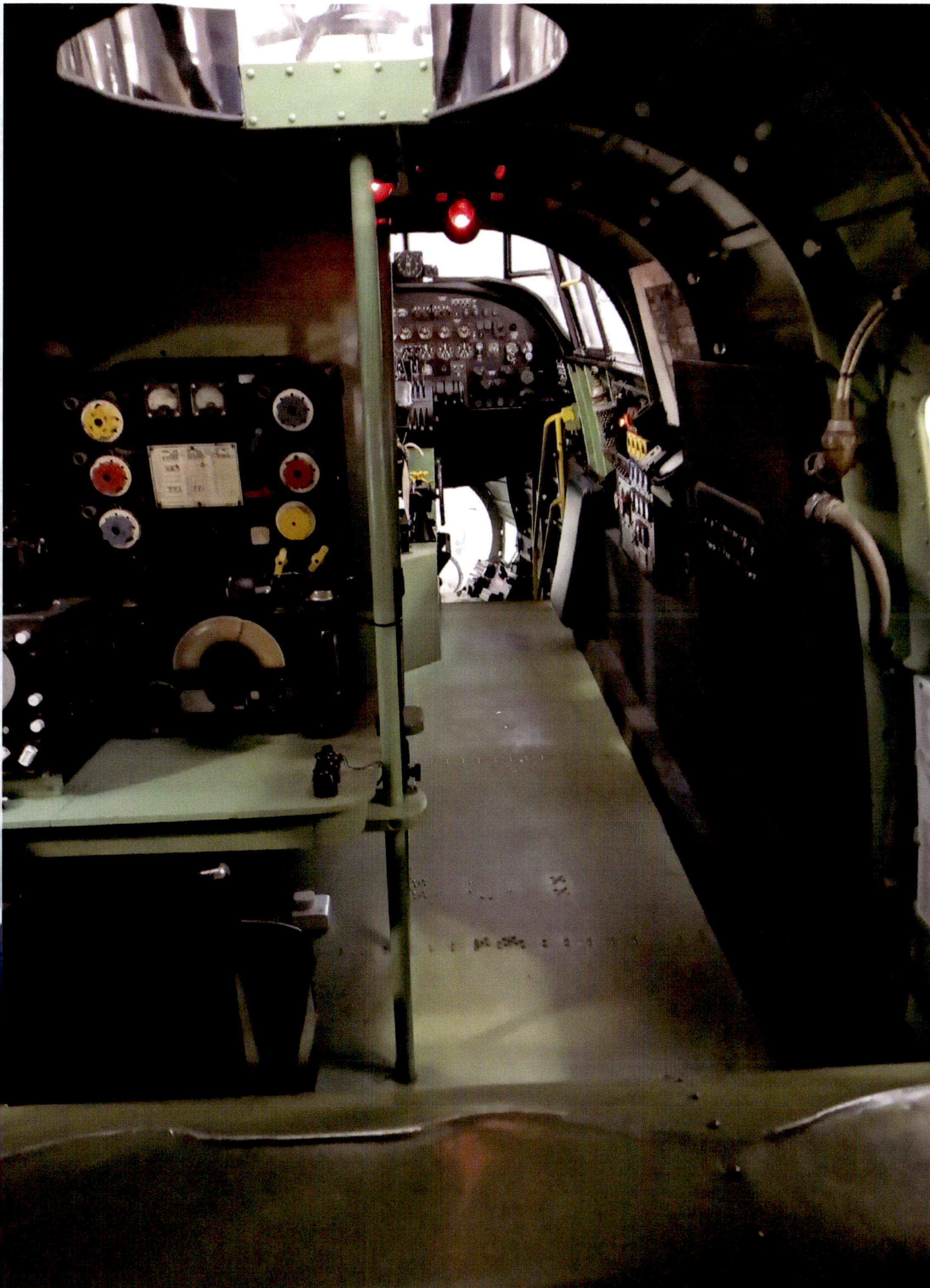

'Gus', as well as my cousins Eric and Jim Bradley, and Henry Lister Simpson all came back wounded in body and in mind. My own grandfather, who served on HMS *Pembroke* and then HMS *Ocean*, refused any 'charity' from the British Legion and I'm not sure I ever saw him wear a poppy. I've never known cocoa quite like the stuff he made: hot, sweet and as thick as fuel oil. He'd gladly talk about his time on *Ocean* in the Med, adventures in Italy, and how they simply dumped failed aircraft over the side as there were no spares, but never spoke of the mess in Greece and the Adriatic coast in 1945, nor being blitzed at Chatham.

Wakefield men and women continue to serve in our armed forces, fighting in the Falklands, Iraq and Afghanistan and serving as peacekeepers. My aunt undertook peacekeeping missions for the UN as part of the Light Infantry and later Intelligence Corps with the Territorial Army. Wakefield has a long association with the armed forces and military. Men and women have lain down their lives for what they believed to be the right thing. A century on from the war to end all wars, the world seems to be more divided than ever. Have we learnt nothing from the millions of lives lost?

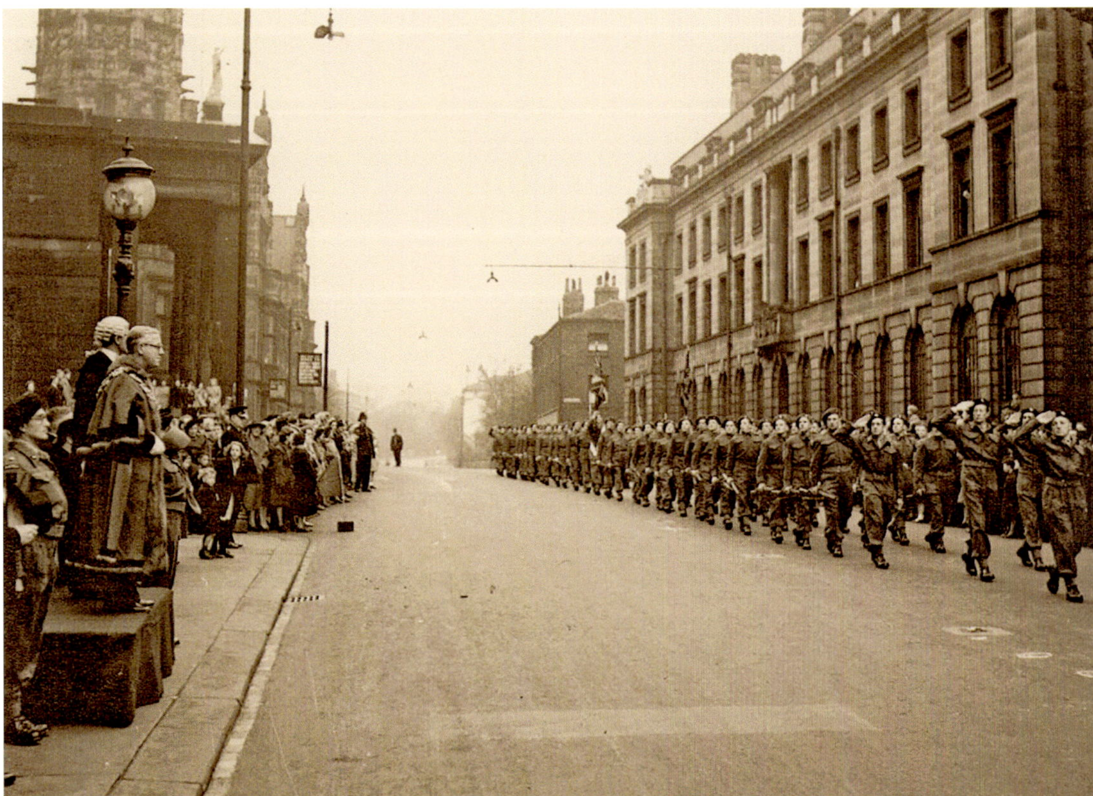

Above and up to page 95: In 1947 the City of Wakefield gave the freedom of the city to Field Marshal Sir Bernard Law Montgomery. At the same ceremony, mayor of Wakefield Councillor Harold Watson presented new colours to the 5th Battalion King's Own Yorkshire Light Infantry. A proud and historic day in the story of our city.

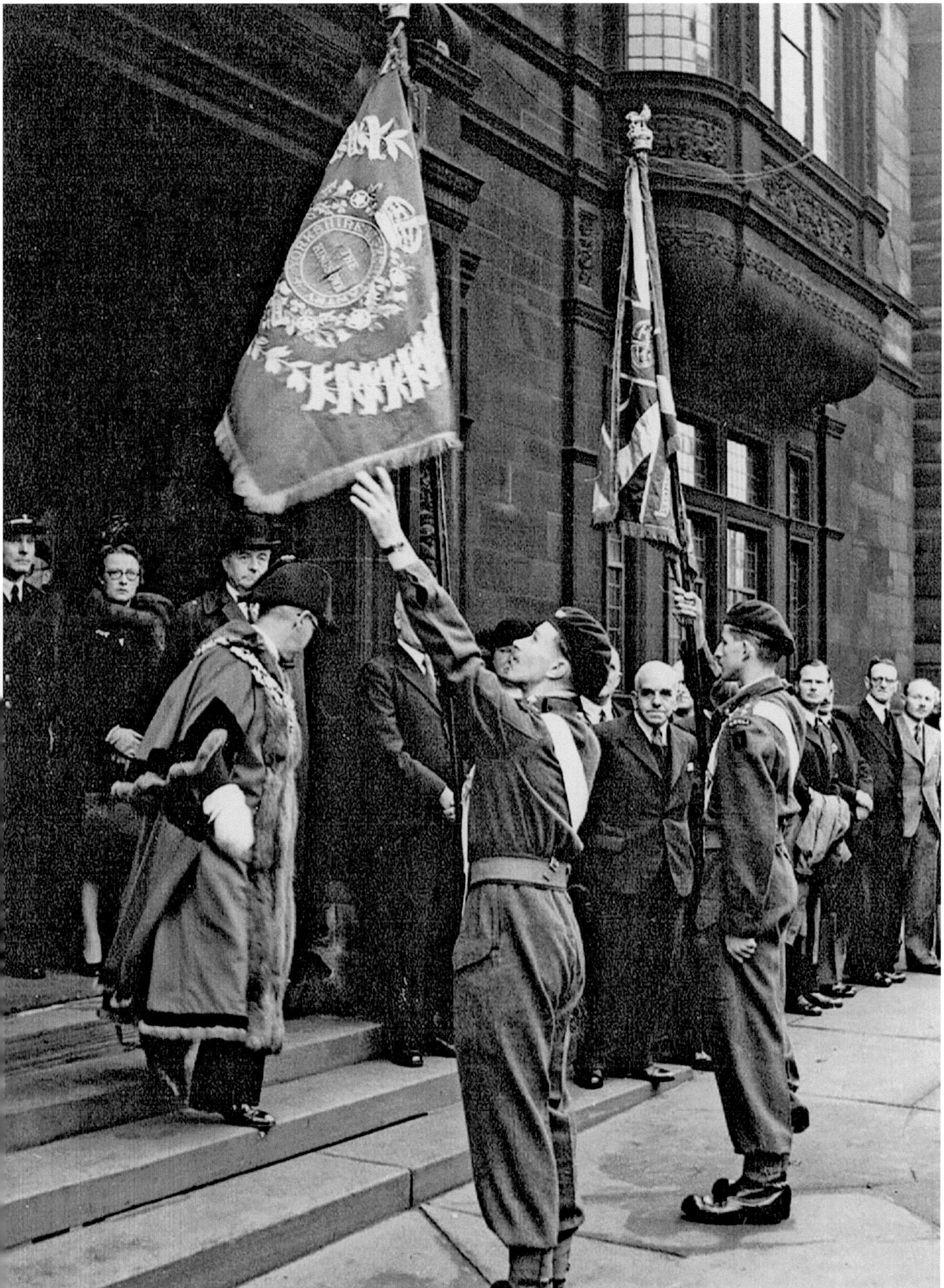

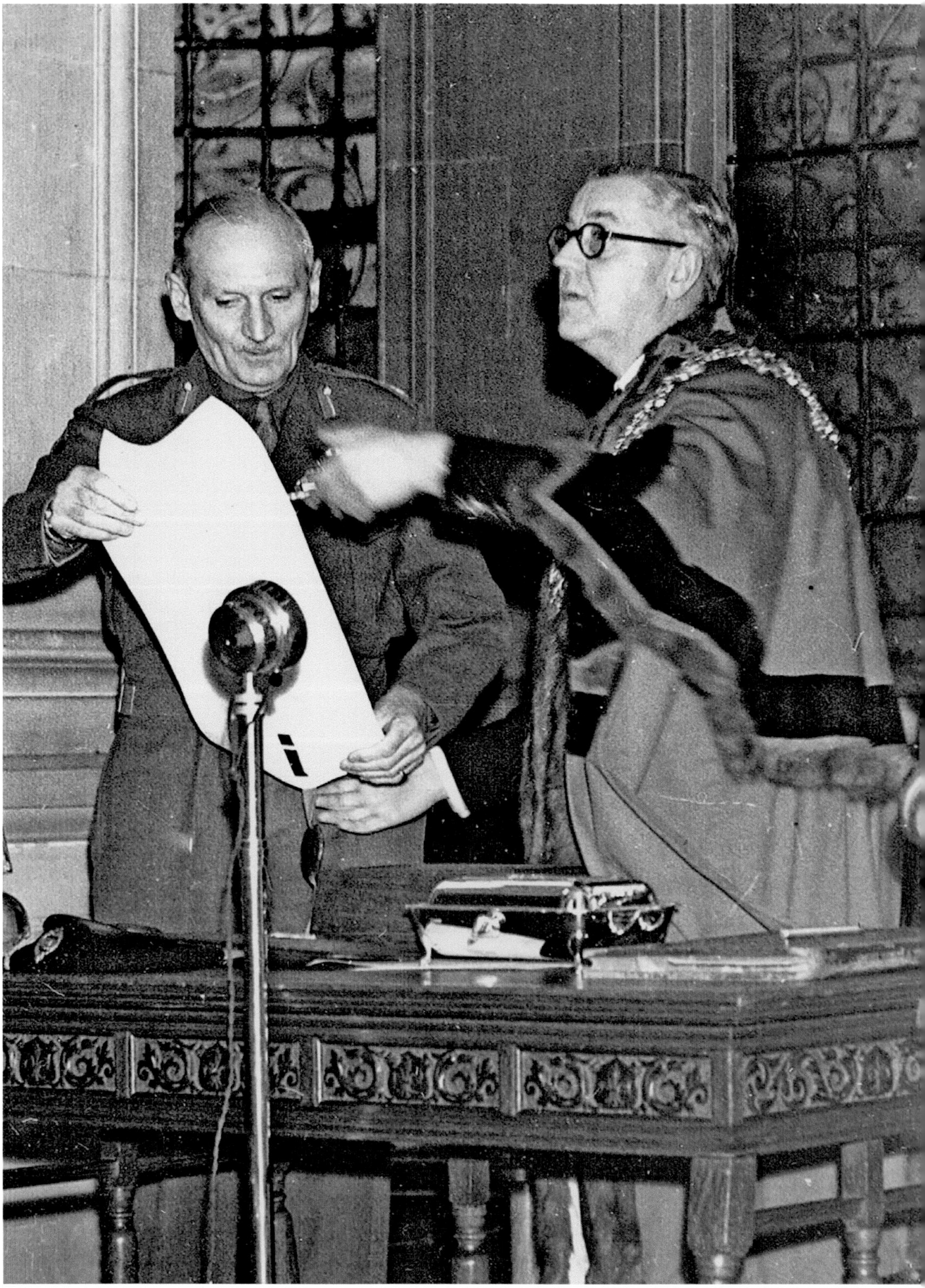

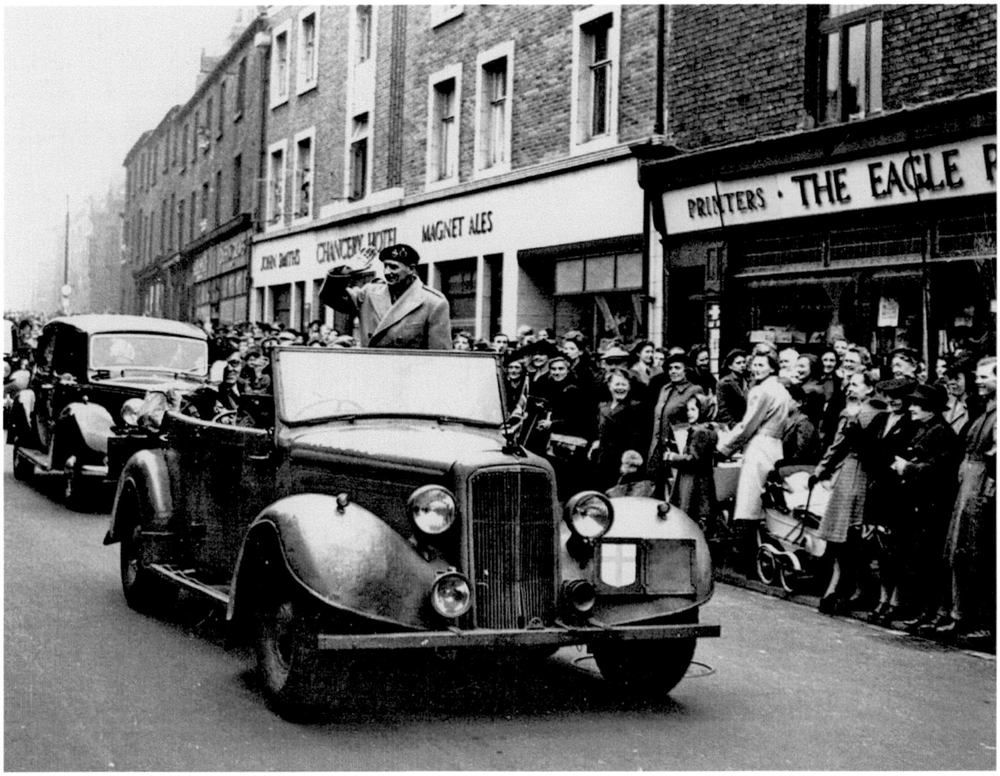
JOHN SMITHS
MAGNET ALES
PRINTERS · THE EAGLE

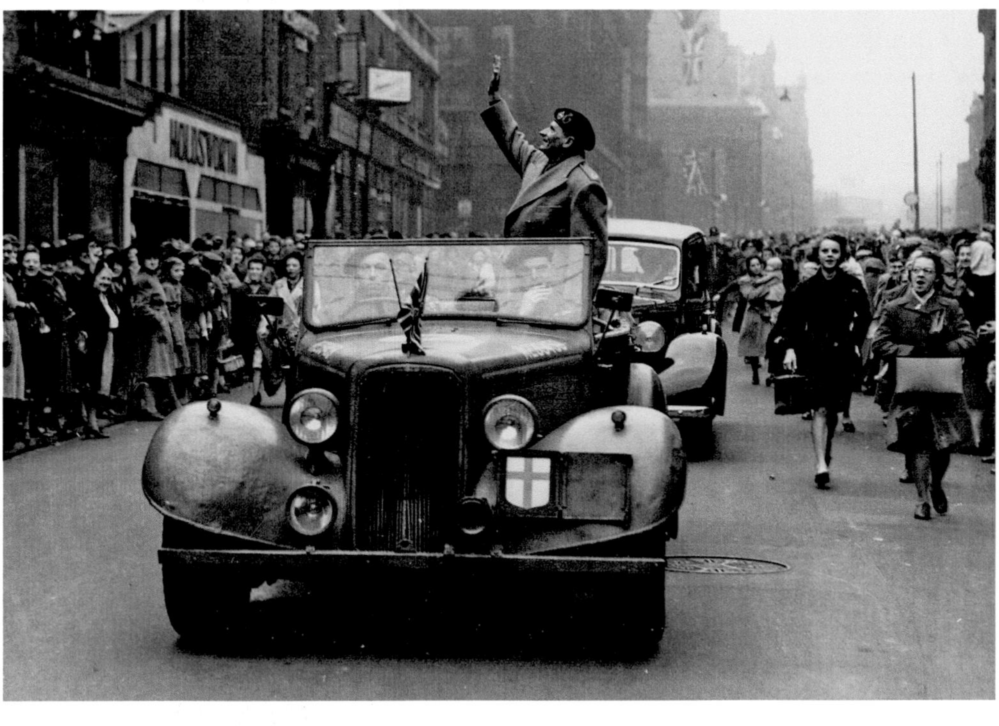

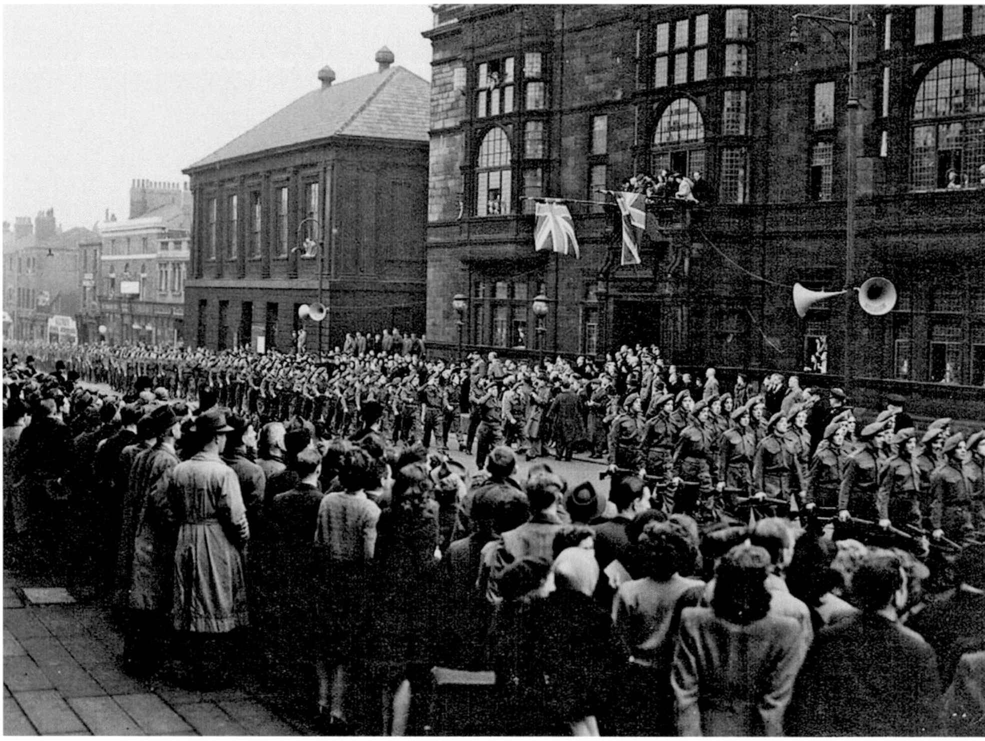

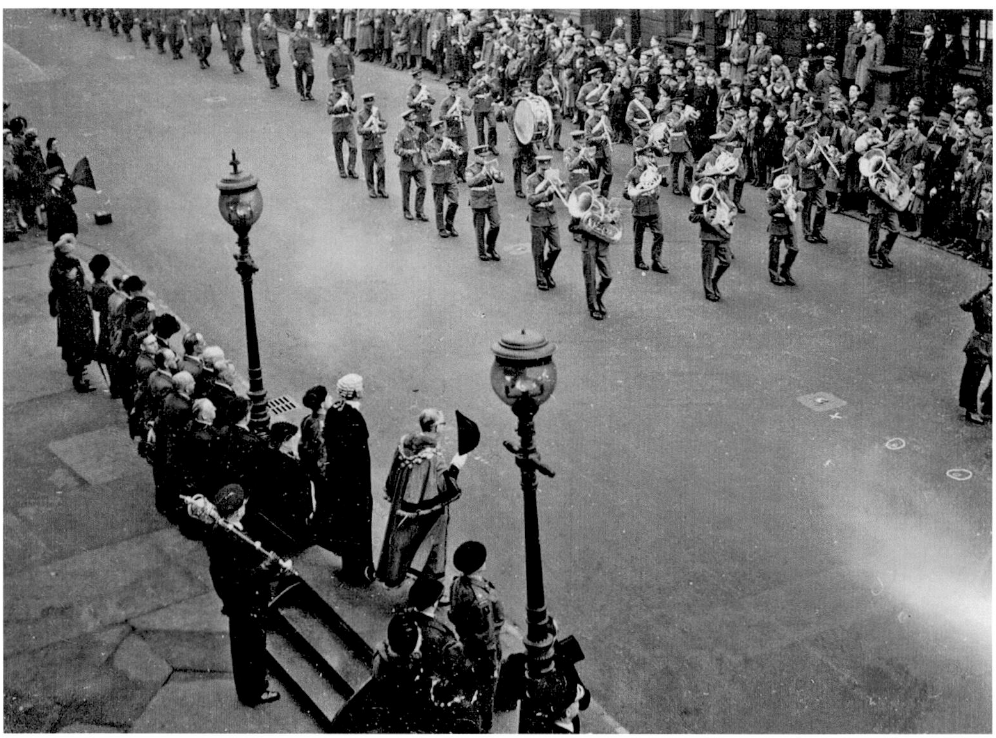

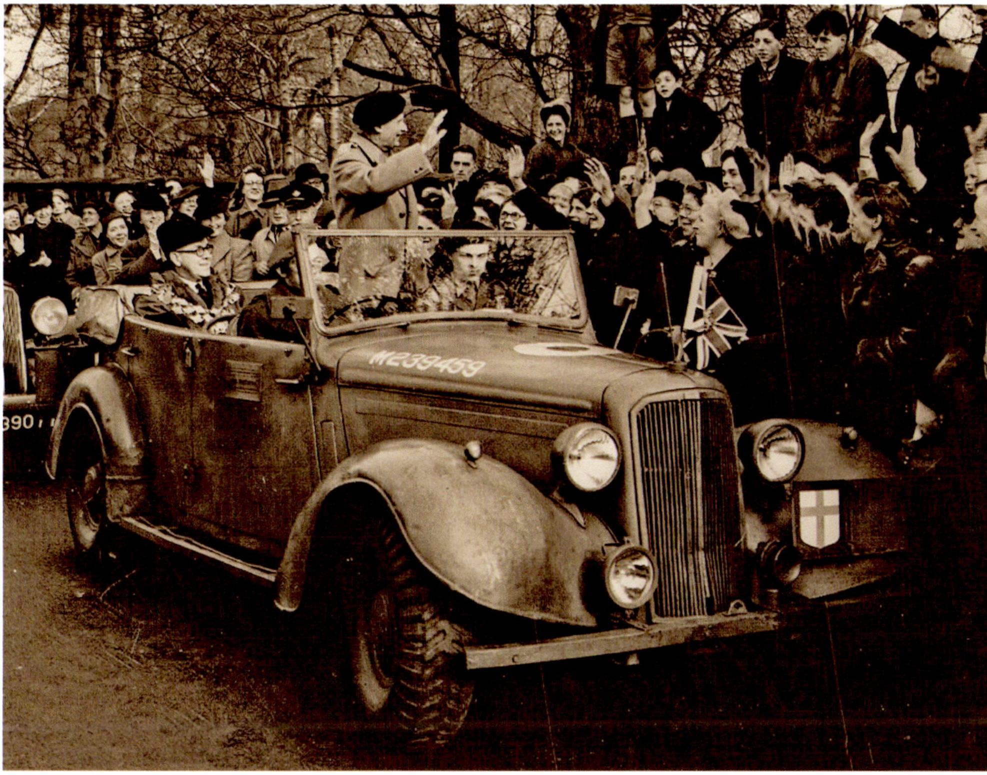
M239459

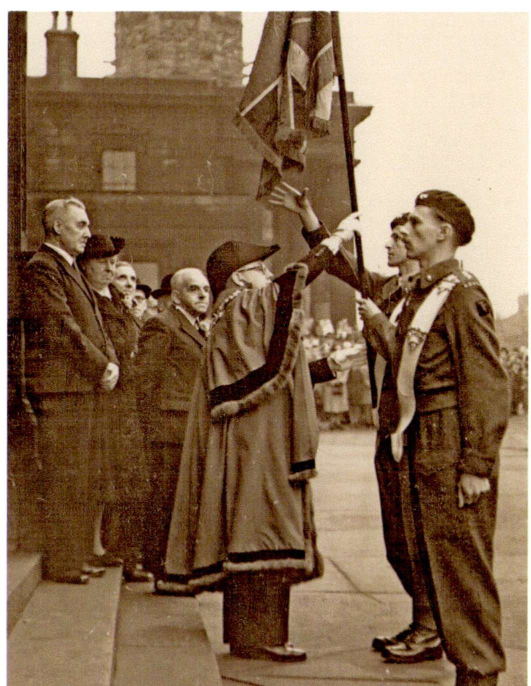

Further Reading

In addition to material held in the John Goodchild collection, the National Archives, Kew, and the West Yorkshire History Centre in Wakefield, the following books will provide useful references for those wanting to know more:

Brears, Peter, *The Buildings of Tudor and Stuart Wakefield* (Wakefield Historical Publications: Wakefield, 2019)

Dawson, Paul Lindsay, *A–Z of Wakefield* (Amberley Publishing, 2019)

Dawson, Paul Lindsay, *Celebrating Wakefield* (Amberley Publishing, 2023)

Dawson, Paul Lindsay, *Changing Wakefield* (Fonthill Media: Stroud, 2015)

Dawson, Paul Lindsay, *Dads Army of the Napoleonic Wars* (Frontline: Barnsley, 2024)

Dawson, Paul Lindsay, *Fighting Napoleon on the Home Font* (Frontline: Barnsley, 2023)

Dawson, Paul Lindsay, *Richard Duke of York: Father of Kings* (Frontline: Barnsley, 2025)

Dawson, Paul Lindsay, *The Battle Against Slavery* (Frontline: Barnsley, 2022)

Dawson, Paul Lindsay, *The Battle Against the Luddites* (Frontline: Barnsley, 2023)

Dawson, Paul Lindsay, *Underground Wakefield* (Amberley Publishing, 2024)

Dawson, Paul Lindsay, *Wakefield: A Potted History* (Amberley Publishing, 2022)

Dawson, Paul Lindsay, *Wakefield at Work* (Amberley Publishing, 2020)

Dawson, Paul Lindsay, *Wakefield Memories* (Sutton: Stroud, 2004)

Taylor, Kate, *The Making of Modern Wakefield* (Wharncliffe: Barnsley, 2008)

Walker, J. W., *Wakefield, Its History and its People* (1934)